The

Impact

of

Identity

—————

THE POWER OF KNOWING
WHO YOU ARE

IRINA NEVZLIN

To my spirited and witty sons, who inspire me to think, question, and learn new things about myself every day.

The Impact of Identity
The power of knowing who you are
Irina Nevzlin

Author's photograph by Yanai Yechiel
Contact: irinanevzlinbook@gmail.com

ISBN 9781698941875

The

Impact

of

Identity

THE POWER OF KNOWING
WHO YOU ARE

IRINA NEVZLIN

Contents

Foreword

I was born, like my daughter, in a country that does not exist anymore. It was called the USSR, and its proclaimed mission was to build the most prosperous and fair state for all the workers in the world. Such words as identity, self-identity, or rootedness, did not exist in the vocabulary of Soviet citizens. "Jewish identity" was an even more exotic expression. Irina writes that she discovered her Jewishness when "someone in my school called me a Jew using a derogatory term." At the same age of seven, I discovered my Jewishness while sneaking a peek at the list of the pupils in my class. I was the only registered Jew! After Irina's discovery, her grandmother told her, "We are not going to say another word about it ever again." Twenty years earlier, my parents basically gave me the same message: it was better not to discuss the fact that we were Jews. For years to follow, my "Jewish identity" included the feeling of being limited in my options for education and my choices for a professional career.

Then, at the end of the '80s, things started to change rapidly. The Soviet Union began to crumble and fall; the old communist doctrine was replaced by the lucrative idea of free enterprise. My life changed dramatically. I began to pursue a professional career in business and, by the end of the '90s, became vice president of the biggest oil company in Russia. I felt like all the doors had begun opening for me. The invisible ceiling I had sensed from my childhood disappeared and the sky was the limit.

Apparently, being a highly successful entrepreneur was not enough for me; I did not want to limit myself to the world of business. When, in 1996, a group of Jewish businessmen and intelligentsia founded the Russian Jewish Congress charitable fund, I felt proud of my "tribesmen" who were not afraid to tell the world they wanted to develop Jewish culture in Russia. I immediately felt a connection to the cause. I began to participate in many of the Congress's projects and to support them financially. Four years later, I was elected the second president of the Congress.

The '90s also played a revolutionary role in forming the Jewish identity of my daughter. In 1992, Irina visited Israel, where she felt at home and underwent an incredible experience at the Western Wall. That same year, she was accepted to the first Jewish school in Moscow, where she discovered: "the same feeling of belonging I had felt in Israel." Actually, my daughter was the first member of my family in three generations to receive a formal Jewish education—something that was absolutely unimaginable in the Soviet Union.

Then things began to change again in Russia. The Soviet Union and KGB began to slowly but surely make their comeback in our lives. My business partner was arrested and I had to leave Russia and move to Israel, while Irina left for England. By that time, my self-identity included not only the feeling of belonging to the Jewish people but the concept of having an active role in Jewish life. Very soon upon arriving in Israel I established the NADAV Foundation, which has been involved in numerous educational and cultural projects in Israel and abroad for the last fifteen years.

For me, one of the happiest moments in my philanthropic career was the day my daughter came to Israel after a short stay in England and decided to join me. She started with a relatively small project of her own, learning the nuts and bolts of philanthropy in Israel, and slowly but surely became more and more involved in other projects and initiatives. Throughout this period, I felt incredible synergy flowing between us. Now, Irina is the president of the NADAV Foundation and the chair of the board of directors of the Museum of the Jewish People—a flagship project of the NADAV Foundation.

For me, this is the continuity and succession of my mission.

For all these years in Israel, both of us have not only been involved in philanthropy, but we have also learned about our family roots. With the help of outstanding Israeli historians, we have managed to dig up our family tree roots back to the end of the 18th century! The realization that you belong to a huge family, and learning the names of hundreds of close and distant relatives, dramatically changes a person's perception of their place and role in this world. You not only realize the uniqueness of yourself, your family, and your people—you also perceive the uniqueness of other individuals, their families, and their people.

I believe this is what happened to Irina. After all, we are not only searching for new definitions of our identity but for new values as well. She came a long way searching for her identity and, during this journey, she discovered inner strength and knowledge that she wanted to share with the world.

The result is her first book, *The Impact of Identity: The power of knowing who you are,* offering tools to forge a multi-faceted identity, rooted in our unique history and experience. It is a guide for people who want to lead a meaningful life in our ever-changing world.

I am very proud of Irina's first book and wish her success in spreading her ideas to the world.

—**Leonid Nevzlin**, *July 2019*

Acknowledgements

This book would have never come to be without the support of my family, friends, partners, and colleagues who have always been there for me.

Special thanks go to my mother and stepfather, for raising me until I took that responsibility upon myself. Also, to my father, who not only endowed me with a passion for exploring the issues of identity but also shares it; our years of deep conversation always ignite my thinking. To my husband Yuli, thank you for listening to all my new ideas at the weirdest times of day and night, and for loving me the way I am. To Tanya, who has been with me for more than half my life and shares much of the experience I describe in this book. To Judith, who helped me believe that Mark Twain was right when he said: "They did not know it was impossible so they did it." To Shelly, who always knows the next step before I do. To Dan, who always manages to succinctly explain what I think. To Alona, for asking deep questions and making me think. And to Misha, for sharing his passion for telling the story of our people.

I would also like to thank the top-notch professionals who helped make this book a reality: Michelle for making it all come together, Chani for spending hours crafting with love, and Sam for taking it to the next level.

Preface

I woke up one morning in December 2018 with a book in my head. Throughout my entire life, until that moment, I had never thought of writing a book but I felt an urge to share a message that derives strictly from personal experience. As Guy Kawasaki says: "Learning by anecdote is risky, but waiting for scientific proof is too."[1]

My message is simple. There are many things we can do and decisions we can make that reduce fear, bring meaning, and enhance enjoyment while exploring life in our fast-changing world.

If you want to make your life better by getting fresh insight and a different perspective—this is the book for you.

Irina Nevzlin

Email: irinanevzlinbook@gmail.com

---

1   Guy Kawasaki, *The Art of the Start 2.0: The Time-Tested, Battle-Hardened Guide for Anyone Starting Anything*, (Old Saybrook: Tantor Media, 2015).

CHAPTER 1

Getting strength from connecting to who you are

In the social jungle of human existence, there is no feeling of being alive without a sense of identity.

— Erik Erikson

Most of us want to have a meaningful life, to be part of something bigger, to feel successful and fulfilled in our life roles—whether as a person, sibling, parent, partner, employee, entrepreneur, volunteer, social activist, citizen, member of society, or simply resident on planet Earth.

But what constitutes a life that has meaning? We want to believe that our life has significance, that we direct our energies into building something we care about. In 1943, Abraham Maslow introduced his hierarchy of needs, where he theorized that humans are hardwired to fulfill basic levels of need—moving onto a new level once they've met the needs of the previous one.[2] We begin with the need to fulfill basic physiological necessities, like food and shelter. Once that is satisfied, we reach up to achieve the higher levels of safety, belonging and love, social esteem, and, ultimately, self-actualization. Life starts to have meaning when you go beyond simply fulfilling your own basic needs.

My journey helped me discover what fosters the strength of spirit needed for a meaningful life. I realized that strength and resilience come from truly understanding and connecting to what makes you, you. Getting to know yourself and your core values is a lifelong process that you can start at any moment. It involves cultivating an honest internal conversation, looking deep inside yourself, and continuously questioning new information and opportunities. Beyond that, it means taking full responsibility for your life, for the answers you give to yourself, and for the choices you make based on these answers.

Why do we need strength and resilience? At times, most of us feel that the world is confusing, scary, and even going downhill. We're uncomfortable with the political, religious, and social changes taking place so quickly. Political extremists and populists are gaining power, fundamentalists are carrying out terror attacks in the name of religion, artificial intelligence is taking over our jobs, and every day the media is blaming someone new for this chaos.

---

2   A. H. Maslow, "A Theory of Human Motivation"; *Psychological Review*, 50, 370-396. (1943)

In truth, things have never been better. Compared to fifty years ago, we have better healthcare, famine is rare, epidemics are quickly curtailed, many parts of the world have clean running water, and equal opportunity is improving all the time. So why do we feel uneasy about what's going on today and so anxious about the future?

I'm not a psychologist or a theoretician. The knowledge and insight I share come directly from my personal experience and years of evaluating what can make you stronger, more resilient, and ready to face whatever the world throws at you.

Born to Jewish parents in communist Russia, growing up when the Iron Curtain fell, and moving from Moscow to London and then to Israel, meant always being an immigrant or in the minority. I continuously examined the cultural norms around me—not by choice, but because I was forced to by my surroundings. I had to try and understand, and often fail to understand, which of them felt right for me, which were not for me, which were mine by birthright, and what exciting new things I could adopt. Being a newcomer immigrant ignited the process of exploring who I was in the most effective way possible—because there was no other option. When you are continuously facing an environment that is outside your comfort zone, you begin asking yourself whether what you know is actually what you like—or just what you know and are used to. This is the process you want to awaken and embrace. True, it's not always comfortable, but on the plus side, you will get to know and enjoy the real you.

Growing up as a minority meant I was compelled to investigate and ask questions so many times that it helped me realize the perspective and accompanying practices shared with you in this book.

What sparked the questions? My family suppressed our Jewish identity. In fact, I didn't even know I was Jewish until the age of seven when someone in my school called me a Jew using a derogatory term. My grandmother, who was a teacher at the school, felt compelled to tell me the truth about my identity. "I am going to tell you two things," she said to me. "There are two Jews in this entire school. You and me. And we are not going to say another word about it ever again." It was a defining moment for me. The next time the topic came up was many years later before a trip to Israel.

The questions didn't end there. I discovered that I was Jewish at seven but nobody would talk to me about it. All I knew was that I was different. Around the same time, I became a member of the Communist Party's young scouts, but shortly afterward when the Iron Curtain fell, I was suddenly no longer a citizen of the USSR. It was a new Russia and no one knew who they were. My identity was blurred before but now became even more so with communism left behind. What did all these new terms and labels mean? Who and what did I connect with?

At thirteen, I notified my parents that I was going to study in a Jewish school. It was time to find like-minded people. This was the first glimmer of taking responsibility for myself.

Later, as a young professional, I immigrated to London and again faced new questions as an outsider to that milieu. And so continued the process of transition, exploration, and asking, "What works for me?"

In this book, I will share with you why it's essential in today's open global world—overflowing with information and opportunities—to understand and connect to who you really are. I will suggest an approach for reaching this understanding, and how to spark the continuous process of asking yourself, "Is this good for me, is this how I do things, or is this just something that is expected of me or something that everyone else does?" Maybe it's not right for you today, this year, or at this time in your life?

Once you become accustomed to boldly asking these questions, you can begin to deal honestly with the answers. Then you can take full responsibly for your life: the opportunities, directions, and ideas you decide to pursue or decline as a result. This is when you stop wasting your life's energy being worried and doing something that is not right for you. You begin to direct this energy toward building a life that has meaning and impact.

WHO AM I?

The authoritarian society into which I was born restricted people's ability to be anyone or anything but a good Soviet citizen. Religion, history, and heritage were wiped out when communism came into play. Everyone had to be equal to be an upstanding member of society. And when everyone is the same, there is no place for individual identity. The many peoples living in the vast USSR region were forced to forget their distinct ethnic identities. They were forbidden to educate their children regarding their history and tradition. They were no longer permitted to practice their religion, own or read books about their background, or preserve their cultural activities. Asking questions was frowned upon as it would only lead to trouble. Today, we are seeing some of the long term effects of how being denied an individual identity has influenced the people in countries such as China, North Korea, or fundamentalist religious states.

Identity is not a static entity or something handed to you for safekeeping. Identity is a process that entails continuously asking, "Who am I?" The importance of your unique identity can't be overstated. All the decisions you make every day of your life, including the most critical and the most superficial ones, are based on how connected you are to who you are and where you're going.

Where did I come from? I was born in 1978, to parents who were Jewish. They knew they were Jewish and, for that, were denied opportunities and treated differently. But that was all they knew. There was no way for them to connect to a Jewish way of life. Citizens were expected to devote their lives to the Soviet state to achieve happiness and fulfillment. In exchange for this devotion, they were given free education, a place to live, food, and other basic needs. Step aside Maslow, we've got it all covered. There was no religious identity, no cultural traditions, and no languages aside from Russian.[3] It was a seventy-year failed attempt to create a Soviet identity by depriving people of their own heritage.

My great-grandparents were religious Jews who spoke only Yiddish. They moved to Moscow and started speaking Russian outside their home, but still spoke Yiddish among themselves. Parents are the ones who are supposed to furnish your first sense of identity and belonging, but my parents were, in some way, displaced. They couldn't get into the university they wanted because they were Jewish, yet they were forbidden to learn what it meant to be Jewish. This is the confusion into which I was born.

At eight-years-old, with black curls and big blue eyes, I was already a member of the Communist Party youth movement. This was the only youth movement around. In fact, it was the only movement or collective anyone was allowed to join. I would go around wearing a pin on my lapel with a portrait of young Lenin—and his curls. At the age of ten, I was a Pioneer in the movement and started wearing a red tie; this was the stage before the Komsomol unit when youngsters are encouraged to become politically active.

In some ways, my friends and I were like any other girls, chattering about boys and making sure people noticed what we were wearing. Except why would someone who reports

---

3   Atlas of the World's Languages in Danger (2010; formerly the Red Book of Endangered Languages) lists over 120 languages spoken in Russia are now vulnerable or on the way to becoming extinct.

their parents to the authorities be so revered that I had to learn his story by heart for school? I remember being taught about Pavlik Morozov, a young Soviet boy who was praised as a martyr. At thirteen years of age, he turned his father in to the authorities for being an enemy of the state. Pavlik was then murdered by his own family, who were subsequently executed. His story had a huge impact and many generations were encouraged to follow his example.

My family was not politically active and was quite happy to stay under the radar. No one ever criticized the Soviet way. It was simply never discussed. My grandmother never joined the Communist Party and was severely restricted in her career opportunities as a result. She was highly intelligent and might have pursued a career other than teaching, but this was not permitted. In fact, my first official job was also as a teacher. To be honest, I was only eighteen and quite miserable teaching young kids economics.

When the Soviet Union collapsed in 1991, I was thirteen years old. Until that time, I had lived a comfortable life and never realized that I was essentially living with a mask on. My parents' world changed completely with the fall of the Soviet Union. There was a new identity in being a citizen of Russia but no one really knew what it meant. Being spiritual became trendy and the Russian Orthodox Church enjoyed a surge of popularity. Former KGB agents became religious, kissing crosses and searching for something to follow. Communism had been the religion and ideology, but when it disappeared people were left with nothing but a void.

My grandmother lived in the same building as us. She was on the third floor and we were on the fifth. There was a relentless parade of odd people coming in and out of her place. These were my grandmother's students, who would bring loads of their belongings and stay over in her tiny apartment. No one ever offered an explanation for their appearance or disappearance. The fact that they struggled for years to preserve their Jewish heritage and were finally going to Israel was known but never discussed. In 1991, shortly after travel outside the country became possible, my grandmother said, "Do you remember my guests? I want to visit them in Israel."

Before we left for Sheremetyevo Airport, my mother sat me down to explain the concept of going abroad. She tried to prepare me for the fact that everything would be unfamiliar, with strange smells, peculiar food, foreign sounds, and odd behavior. I had no idea what to expect. After landing, my grandmother and I went to stay with a family in the city of Rehovot, near the center of the country. I was amazed to see food in the street and the smell wafting out of the pizza shop was like heaven on earth. I felt strangely comfortable and completely at home. I realized that I had been living with a permanent sense of unease. How bizarre that the first time I really felt at home was in Israel, with a strange family, in a place where I had never been before.

One day, my grandmother announced that we were going to the Kotel, the Western Wall. The Kotel in Jerusalem is the last remnant of the Holy Temple and probably the most significant site in the world for the Jewish people. People from around the world gather at the wall to pray, connect to their history, and write notes they cram in between the ancient stones. At the time, I had no idea of its importance and no knowledge about the history of the Jewish people. All I knew at that point could be summed up in the fact that I was different. Still, when we reached the Kotel, I went through an intense personal experience that triggered something very integral inside me. I cried for hours—and crying is absolutely not part of my personality. It was like meeting someone I never knew before and sensing an instant true and deep bond. This defining moment and deep connection with the Kotel is difficult to explain intellectually.

In Russia, I had to put on "armor" before going outside the house, but in Israel, I felt I could be the same inside and outside on the street. I had never eaten hummus or pita before and couldn't understand why everyone was always shouting. I had never stayed in someone else's house before, yet here I was living with strangers and feeling more at home than I ever had back in Moscow.

I grew up in a working-class neighborhood with friends who started drinking at the age of twelve. No one was really keen on school and many of them ended up in jail at some point. My parents sent me for private English lessons and impressed on me that doing well in English and math was a top priority. How was it possible that I had come to the Middle East, where people spoke Hebrew, everything was unfamiliar, and yet it felt like I belonged?

When I got back to Moscow, a friend contacted me and asked if I would be interested in visiting his new school. He described it as a place where "our people" study—but, at the time, I didn't really get what he meant. He and I had gone through nursery together and had sat side by side at the same desk in class for six years, until one day he disappeared. It turned out he had joined the Jewish school the year it opened. Unlike my family, his talked about being Jewish and what it meant. Little did I know that this invitation would change my life. I went along to have a look at the school without telling my parents. When we arrived, I was told it was the day of the school's entrance exams. This was a practice unheard of in Russia, yet I found myself crouched over a desk writing exams in every subject for the entire day.

The next day, the school called to say I was one of seven people out of eighty who were accepted for studies in the coming year. I bravely announced to my parents that I was moving schools. They, of course, firmly opposed the idea. It was far from home and they didn't want me studying at a Jewish school for security reasons. Very quickly, they realized they were done making the decisions for me. I was taking responsibility and letting them know my plans.

The school was a crucial turning point for the identity I was now forming. When I began studying at the school, I was amazed to discover the same feeling of belonging I had sensed in Israel. Everyone knew English and everyone was thinking about moving to another country. My new friends were ambitious and armed with a deprecating self-humor.

No longer feeling isolated, I had the strength and support I needed to grow in new directions. I learned about my people, Jewish history, and Zionism instead of children who reported their parents to the authorities.

Being part of a people is not a superficial identity. Nor is it a label you apply, like liberal, musician, vegan, or businessman. It's something essential you are born into and a deep part of you that will never change. Knowing who your people are and being part of a community allows you to develop a stronger connection to your roots. This sense of belonging to something bigger and deeper—that has always been there for you—and the notion of being stronger together is what I want to help you achieve.

Connecting to your ancestors is not about obligations or religious beliefs. Each small part of your roots—whether place, tradition, history, culture, or language—is something that can be appreciated (or not) and incorporated (or not) on its own. If you can see each of these clearly and individually, you will be able to decide what works for you. For me, belief is an internal spiritual entity. I don't feel the need to follow the rules of organized religion. Then again, the tradition itself has a more flexible role in my life. I'm not a history buff so that is not where I connect, but culture is important to me, as is the land. The bottom line is that, once you have more information, you are free to pick and choose.

I like the freedom of connecting to my roots in a way that meshes comfortably with my lifestyle and philosophies. You can be an atheist and still find it meaningful to celebrate holidays, light candles, listen to music, or eat traditional foods. In my own family, each of us has a unique outlook. One of my sons loves Jewish rituals like blessing the wine on Friday night and having a big family meal. My other son doesn't see any point in it, but my husband is very connected to religious observance and practices. It's not about belief in God or religious observance. The starting point for building inner strength lies in connecting to your roots and your people. Whatever works for you personally is the right thing to do.

Connecting to my Jewish roots empowered me and is what ultimately led me to become involved in transforming the Museum of the Jewish People in Tel Aviv, as discussed later in the book. For now, let's backtrack to my school years. I graduated high school, went to Moscow State University to get my bachelor's and master's degrees in economics, and then started working in public relations and strategic communications. By this time, I had distinct circles of friends— my professional sphere and my "brothers and sisters" from school.

In 1999, Vladimir Putin rose to power and, in 2003, Michael Khodorkovsky was thrown into prison. Khodorkovsky was the visionary behind the Yukos oil company and my father's partner. It was a politically motivated arrest and Moscow ceased to be a city where I wanted to live. I decided to move to London so I could continue working in an international, English-speaking, environment. Fortunately, the company where I worked had an office in London and was able to transfer my position. This was yet another turning point in understanding how identity influences a person's life.

Living in London as a new immigrant, I found myself feeling naked. In this new situation, I began questioning everything I knew about myself. When everyone and everything around you is shouting "you are different," you try to understand why. Asking "why" is one of the skills I want to share with you in this book. You don't have to undergo an uncomfortable transition to begin asking these questions. It can be an ongoing process, ideally taught as a way of life and part of our family values or educational skills.

The questions kept floating up to the surface. The distance from my friends in Moscow gave me a different perspective on these relationships. Were they my soul mates or friends simply because we worked together as colleagues? Did I really miss the Russian borscht and pirozhki or was it just what I was used to eating? I needed to filter out what I enjoyed from my old culture and what I wanted to adopt from the new. Who knew I would become a fan of live jazz performances? Being an outsider helps you ask and answer these questions more honestly because you are not assuming you have to be part of some social norm. The good news is that you don't have to be an outsider to start questioning.

The first Friday in the London office had me swamped with back to back meetings when a fellow named Jon came over and asked, "what are you doing Friday night?" I had no idea if he was Jewish or not, but he knew I was. His first reaction to the new Jewish girl in town was to invite me over for Friday night dinner, simply because I was a member of his tribe. As a newcomer, this made an indelible impression. Who knew that being Jewish gave me instant membership to an international network? The nation you come from is a resource that you belong to and that belongs to you. I was no longer alone.

This membership was an enormous asset. I could call a Jewish board member of the company we were working with, introduce myself, and say "what's going on, I'm new in town, what should I look into?" And instantly, we were "friends." I now had a new acquaintance who was ready to share advice. In fact, I'm still in touch with many of these contacts today. Having a ready-made network based on a shared background is something that most immigrants enjoy—including Italian, Lebanese, Estonian, Irish, Nigerian and many others.

When you belong to a majority sector, you don't think about this resource. Jews who grow up in Israel can't fathom that they are part of a network with fifteen million people around the world.[4] To say nothing of the Scottish people who claim

---

4   "World Jewish Population, 2017," Berman Jewish DataBank, https://www.jewishdatabank.org/content/upload/bjdb/World_Jewish_Population_2017_AJYB_DataBank_Final.pdf

as many as a hundred million across the globe.[5] This has nothing to do with politics, belief, or way of life. This membership exists, whether or not you feel connected to your own people. Even if you don't really feel comfortable with your people, you can choose to ignore the community, but you need to understand this connection. It is the deepest part of your identity and something that will never change. You are stronger when you know who you are and are connected to your ethnic heritage.

After three fast-paced years in London, I had gained professional experience and built a rich network of friends and contacts. It was a fascinating period, offering incredible experiences and many opportunities to learn. Then, it was time to move to Israel. The decision was not something I made on an intellectual level, although I knew London was not home and felt I had reached my maximum potential there. Throughout my time in London, my connection to Israel remained strong. My father had moved to Tel Aviv a few years before and I would fly over to visit every few months. In 2006, life in Russia had again become uneasy. When my mother decided to move to Israel, I booked a flight so I could help her. It was there, on British Airways Flight 164, the horrible red-eye that never leaves you enough time to sleep, as my mind started drifting, that I knew that it was time to go home.

---

5   Chris McCall, "The Scottish diaspora: How Scots spread across the globe," *The Scotsman*, January 25, 2016, https://www.scotsman.com/news/the-scottish-diaspora-how-scots-spread-across-the-globe-1-4011012]

Once my decision was made, I spent three intense months wrapping up work with my clients in London and then immigrated to Israel. My first order of business was to find a job. How would I continue building my career in a country where my grasp of the language was barely adequate and the concept of long-term planning was low on everyone's list of priorities? It was full-on survival mode. I went from crafting media training and image-building with executives from Phillip Morris and Microsoft to being offered a job with three Russian-language journalists in Israel. My work experience was clearly not adaptable.

Although visiting Israel was something I had relished for years, it was a real eye-opener to live in the country as a resident. Why am I constantly being jostled in the street by people who never apologize? Why does the taxi driver yell when I need change for a fifty? Are basic manners and courtesy irrelevant? Why does the woman behind me in the supermarket line feel comfortable asking whether I'm married and what my salary is? Or telling me how many kids I should be having? Once again, I was the outsider and the old question marks began popping up—just under different circumstances. What are my political views? Do I have any? Why am I friends with this group? What do I enjoy doing in my free time? What has priority in my life? My new "home" was very different from what I had envisioned.

Parallel to searching for a job, I was busy volunteering and studying Hebrew at Tel Aviv University. I didn't have the luxury of saying, "Oh, I'm not good with languages." In today's open world, you can't flourish without at least one additional language. As soon as people heard my accent, they were eager to practice their English. I realized that I needed to do myself the favor of learning the new language rather than indulging them; I began asking people not to speak to me in English. It took about two years until I really understood what people were saying, even though I pretended to understand everything so they wouldn't revert to English.

Helping my father with our family's philanthropic projects gave me the opportunity to build the Israeli Center for Better Childhood and initiate other not-for-profit projects. At the time, my father encouraged me to join a meeting of the Diaspora Museum, which he supported as a result of then Prime Minister Ariel Sharon's plea to help save the museum. Sharon felt it was important for Israelis to know their history and was adamant that the Jewish people have a place that told their story. My father agreed to help just a bit, and then a bit more, and then he gave them me. I was at a meeting when the board of directors took on the difficult question of whether or not the museum had a future. Someone from our family foundation team pointed out that the museum would have a future if it moved from preserving history to telling the story of the Jewish people then and now. That statement was the bug that bit me—I had finally found a way to share with others how meaningful it is to be Jewish and part of your people.

I went from being a representative of the foundation, to an observer on the board of directors, a member of the board, the deputy chair of the board, and finally, to the active chair of the newly transformed Museum of the Jewish People. It became my goal to make over the museum so it told the story of the Jewish people—because that's the story of my life. The museum's goal is to strengthen people's identity by helping them understand and connect to who they are. In keeping with this way of thinking, the goal of this book is to help you become more resilient by igniting the process of asking: Who am I, what is my unique heritage, and what gives my life meaning?

TREES, ROOTS, AND PERSONAL GROWTH

He will be like a tree planted near water, which spreads out its roots along a brook and does not see when heat comes, whose foliage is ever fresh; it will not worry in a year of drought and will not stop producing fruit.

Jeremiah 17: 8

Humans are compared to trees in many quotes and proverbs. The tree starts with roots below the ground, drawing nutrients to help it flourish. As the roots grow stronger, the trunk gets taller, thicker, and sturdier until new branches can sprout. These ultimately support new branches, which spread to grow leaves, fruit, or flowers. The ideal tree has strong branches covered with rich greenery. But for all this to happen, you need strong roots. The roots of our family and our people give us a solid foundation and the strength we need to branch out and face the world.

Like the tree, humans remain fragile without nurturing anchoring roots. When we're not connected to our roots, we are essentially rootless, floating, desperately grasping onto one affiliation or another. Without working from a true understanding of and connection to what makes us who we are, we end up feeling threatened by views or lifestyles that are different and condemning others. Being rooted is a prerequisite for being resilient and open-minded.

Each of us was born somewhere and to someone. Your history is a rich collection of parents, ancestors, countries, languages, cultures—all part of who you are. Whether you know about it or not, it's yours. If you connect to your roots, it can make you stronger, like the tree.

This history is part of your identity and is a fact that will not change. You might like your roots, and feel connected to them, or decide to ignore them. Either way, it's vital to ask questions and find out where you came from—even if you decide that it doesn't suit you. It's part of who you are.

When you have a true fundamental grasp of your own identity, you'll face the world with more confidence and resilience. Identity is not something static; it's a fluid process to be nurtured, cultivated, and cherished. This book is about understanding and shaping your identity so you can lead a life with meaning. Starting now.

CHAPTER 2

Why post-2000 feels unnerving

Life is suffering. We can only bear it if it has meaning. And meaning is created when you take responsibility – by confronting hardship and firmly steering your ship forward, even against waves that will, ultimately, overwhelm it. This is a message people are "hungry for" in our times.

— **Jordan B. Peterson**

In the past, life was simpler and more static. You knew who you were, where you were likely to live when you grew up, what sort of career you'd have, and it wasn't all that different from how your parents or grandparents lived. Your value system generally came from religious leaders, politicians, or newspapers, all of which were more or less local to the environment. These "elites" defined our views and opinions and, of course, our subsequent beliefs and actions.

Starting from the year 2000, the internet transitioned from academia and the military to everyone's desktop and, later, onto our mobile devices. This sparked a process that opened countless new channels of information. Going beyond the revolution that took place when Gutenberg invented the printing press, today anyone can instantly publish news to the entire world. As a result, we are forced to filter the deluge of information directed at us. Does WikiLeaks now define what you know or believe as opposed to the *Wall Street Journal* or *The Times*?

With the explosion of the internet into our daily lives, "who we are" is heavily influenced by a whole load of parties and channels that provide continuous input: politicians, media, religious leaders, academic elite—even security profession- als. It can be anyone and everyone who creates a news web- site, blog, or other media channel.

The definitions and identities we embraced for years are no longer stable. They are changing quickly and continuously. Gender is no longer limited to man or woman. The farm- er in western Canada faces competition from growers in China. The helpdesk technician may wonder if her job will be moved to a customer support facility in India. Left, right, Democrat, and Republican no longer have the same mean- ing. Street protesters become members of parliament. What is more, every media outlet is propounding who is to blame for this chaos. Is anyone comfortable with so much change?

We're being swamped with new options for identities, labels, and communities we should associate with or even join. This makes our outlook on the world more complex and downright daunting for two reasons. First, there are so many more ways to think of identity that the identities themselves become diluted. Second, the foundations, structures, and value systems built on these identities have undergone so much change that they are no longer valid.

MAKING SENSE OF THE WORLD TODAY

Imagine that you wake up and find a notice in your mailbox stating that the city zoning laws have been restructured and your street is part of a new township. Most of us would feel an immediate sense of unease. Others—although a minority—might embrace the change and feel excited for a chance to leave their comfort zone.

When uncertainty caused by so many changes leaves us feeling uneasy and confused, we begin to hear statements like: "I don't understand what's going on in the world today" or "the world is going nuts." The response to this is inevitably: "We have to turn the clock back to when things were good." The problem is that we live in the present. Despite the fact that each generation tends to feel things were better in the old days, research shows that our standard of living, well-being, and happiness are only going up.

Truth be told, this same feeling of unease is what sparked my journey in search of answers. I was determined to move from surviving to living. It was time to start having some serious conversations with myself, understand what was causing my inner sense of conflict, examine the evidence, and realize that I was responsible for any attitudes, changes, and decisions.

Sometimes you just need to recognize your apprehension, observe what is going on, try to figure out why you are uneasy, and move on from there. Only then can the panic dissipate. This message, so elegantly explained by Eckhardt Tolle in his book *Practicing the Power of Now*, is something I try to bear in mind: "All you really need to do is accept this moment fully. You are then at ease in the here and now and at ease with yourself."[6]

This feeling of unease in a "messed up" world is aggravated by a number of factors that we'll look at together later in this chapter. First, in the era of the internet and social media, our identities have become much harder to define, connected, as most of us are, to 1.8 billion Facebook "citizens," among numerous other social media. Second, people are rebelling against the past century's dominant, liberal dogma to view everyone as the same, treat everyone identically, and distribute everything equitably. As a reaction, more and more voices are focusing on what divides us, whether political leanings, race, economic status, or ethnic origins. We're seeing clear evidence of this in the rise of right-wing conservatism, Brexit, and the battles of religious fundamentalists. Third, the same drive encouraging everyone to be citizens of the world is pushing us to ignore the core of our identity—our tribe—the people we were born into. Although you can change the language you speak, the country you live in, or even your gender, you cannot change your origins. Who

6   Eckhardt Tolle, Practicing the Power of Now, Vancouver: Namaste Publishing, 2004

your people are will remain an integral part of your identity throughout your entire life.

We are both constrained and enriched by our origin and tribe. But within this greater collective identity, there lies our personal identity; this defines who you are and what is right for you as an individual. Unless you feel confident that it is you who gets to decide how you live your life, you will be hard-pressed to face information and opinions coming at you from the outside. My goal is to offer the skills you need to understand who you are, practically and philosophically. When you feel free to make your own choices, you are in control and will no longer feel frustrated by outside forces inundating you with new information, opinions, labels, and identities.

Let's take a closer look at these factors, how they developed over the last centuries, and why they affect us as they do.

WHAT BROUGHT ON THESE NEW DEFINITIONS, STRUCTURES, AND IDENTITIES?

This is not the first time in history that progress and change have brought on a wave of unease and anxiety regarding the future. We'll take a closer look at other periods of enormous change, including the Scientific Revolution, the Modern Agricultural Revolution,[7] and the Industrial Revolution.

---

7   Also known as the second Agricultural Revolution, after the initial one that changed mankind from hunter-gatherers to farmers.

It will then become clear why contemporary mass globalization—part of the Information and Communication Revolution—feels so threatening.

A CLOSER LOOK AT THE SCIENTIFIC REVOLUTION

The Scientific Revolution started in the late sixteenth century and continued to the early eighteenth century in Europe.[8] We know it as the period of unprecedented ideas and discoveries in physics, astronomy, biology, chemistry, human anatomy, and other sciences. It's easy to forget that this Revolution also resulted in people rejecting the dogmata and beliefs that had been prevalent since ancient Greece.

The new science was brought about through exploration and new discoveries. All of it was sparked by people who boldly questioned established authority and ideas to gain new knowledge. It changed the way people viewed the world and their place in it. It laid the foundation of modern science as we know it—a synergy of questions, discussions, experiments, and ensuing knowledge.

Most experts agree that the Scientific Revolution got underway when Nicolaus Copernicus proclaimed that the earth and the other planets revolve around the sun. He was also

8   "Scientific Revolution," Stephen G. Brush et al., *Encyclopedia Britannica*, last modified May 3, 2019, https://www.britannica.com/science/Scientific-Revolution and "Physical science," J. Brookes Spencer et al., *Encyclopedia Britannica*, last modified December 13, 2018, https://www.britannica.com/science/physical-science#ref406942

the first scientist to state that the earth rotates on its axis over a twenty-four-hour period. This was completely radical, coming at a time when people were convinced the earth stood still in the center of the universe and everything else revolved around it. In short, he shook the foundations of society by saying the universe did not work as previously thought, our earth was not at the center, and religious leaders had it wrong for centuries.

The Scientific Revolution was a big shake up for the Church, which served as the predominant purveyor of values and knowledge. Moreover, because the Roman Catholic Church had established the universities, there was now conflict, and not only partnership, between science and religion.

Did the general population feel the same unease we do today, with fresh technology popping up on a daily basis? Elite intellectuals slowly absorbed the new beliefs and knowledge, but they had the advantage of education and could more easily grasp these new concepts. The masses didn't have the resources to absorb or accommodate the new ways of thinking. When the revelations of the Scientific Revolution starting trickling into their lives, many people naturally reacted with fear and mistrust.

Most people were concerned with their livelihood, family, and quality of life. They weren't eager to question long-established beliefs, preferring to maintain the traditional opinions and views also held by their neighbors or the people they met at church. The influence of the Church and the traditions that had been passed down for hundreds of years represented a formidable mystical power that offered answers for any adversity life brought to their doorstep. Things didn't happen because of gravity or mechanical forces, they were caused by the positioning of the planets or God. The belief in astrology, ghosts, and magic continued well into the nineteenth century, even among some of the ruling class and nobles.

In *The Structure of Scientific Revolutions* by Thomas Kuhn, published in 1962, one of the seminal texts about scientific advances in general, Kuhn elegantly stated that scientific revolutions are those singular episodes in which an older paradigm is replaced in whole or part by an incompatible new one.[9] These paradigms, or accepted ways of thinking and doing, are exactly what is changing in our times. We trust these ways of thinking, which are essentially convictions and beliefs in the way things work. We rely on these convictions to stay calm, solve problems, or know how to react and behave. When the old definitions are no longer valid, it's like having the rug pulled out from under us. The old paradigms can no longer be used as guides or standards. This is exactly the time to start asking questions: what makes me feel uneasy, what are my options, what do I choose or not choose to do now?

What sparked the Scientific Revolution? It wasn't Copernicus's revelation but rather the fact that he and others

---

9   Thomas S. Kuhn, ed., *The Structure of Scientific Revolutions*, 3rd edition, (Chicago: University of Chicago Press, 1996).

such as Galileo, Newton, Kepler, and Bacon began asking questions and seeking answers. To learn more about yourself and the world around you, you need to examine what is going on—including the paradigms—and ask questions about why things work the way they do, what works for me, and what doesn't.

DID THE INDUSTRIAL REVOLUTION HAVE A SIMILAR EFFECT?

The Industrial Revolution began in the late 1700s when the advent of steam power and the cotton gin launched the production of manufactured goods in factories. This had a dramatic impact on people's lives in a number of ways. Up until then, you could basically eat or use what you grew or made at home or got from your neighbor. Many people began moving from rural areas to big cities where new jobs had become available. The greater availability of transportation meant people and goods could travel around the country or the world by railroad, by steamboat, or, by the late nineteenth century, by automobile. Once businesses began to use the new technological advances such as electricity, production lines, and steel processing, things shifted even more.

Think about how these enormous waves of change affected people's lives and attitudes. Before the Revolution, rural areas or farms were what most people called home. With the move to the cities, populations grew at an unprecedented rate, reshaping society. There was a new urban middle class that made demands from the government and insisted on having a say in how their lives were governed. People's thoughts moved beyond getting enough food to fill their stomachs. There was a new understanding of the world, new countries to visit, and new forms of government.

Despite the upheaval in their daily lives, things had never been better for the general population. Sound familiar? Printers began to use steam power to print books and newspapers cheaply, allowing more people than ever to read and be informed—leading to demands for universal education. Practical inventions like the telegraph, sewing machine, and light bulb extended people's days and ability to communicate or create. Because it now took four hours to get from London to Manchester instead of four days, people, goods, and food arrived faster. Fresh milk and letter writing turned into daily habits. And, of course, the new industries created jobs, which meant wages earned, bringing people more wealth and giving the economy a big push. It was an enormous change that reset all previous paradigms.

Although many people were uncomfortable with the changes brought on by the Industrial Revolution, its ensuing technological advances marked the first time in history that humans enjoyed a dramatic leap in their quality of life and well-being. The Revolution brought jobs and food, the ability to make a living, childhood education that started in factories and then moved to the schools, travel, and more. I see the impact of the Information and Communication Revolution that we're living through as being at least of the same magnitude. We'll discuss that soon.

This gives us a sense of historical perspective. But how did the people feel? In 1845, German philosopher Friedrich Engels spent two years studying the living conditions in Manchester and misdirected historians thereafter when he published *The Condition of the Working Class in England*.[10] Apart from duly impressing Karl Marx, the book's description of terrible suffering and spiritual loss set the stage for other historians to portray the Industrial Revolution as a tragedy for the working class. As articulated by Amanda Vickery in *The Guardian*: "This fable of proletarian immiseration underscored left-leaning history thereafter."[11]

Despite the historically popular attitude that people were wretched as a result of the unbearable work conditions in the factories, many of them were actually better off than before. Vickery's article reviews the book *Liberty's Dawn* by Emma Griffin[12] that offers a completely different take based on 350 published and unpublished autobiographies of working people. The bottom line of the collection is that the ordinary worker enjoyed a healthier and less stressful life than before the Industrial Revolution, when living on the farm and vulnerable to the whims of Mother Nature.

10   Friedrich Engels, *The Condition of the Working Class in England,* Translated, (Germany: Otto Wigand, 1845).

11   Amanda Vickery, "Liberty's Dawn: A People's History of the Industrial Revolution by Emma Griffin—review," *The Guardian*, December 26, 2013, https://www.theguardian.com/books/2013/dec/26/libertys-dawn-emma-griffin-review

12   Emma Griffin, *Liberty's Dawn: A People's History of the Industrial Revolution,* (New Haven: Yale University Press, 2014).

I found this article intriguing because it typifies how the story gets warped with the telling. We can see how certain "loud voices" demonized the government and new businesses and blamed them for turning the general population into victims of the new technology. Likewise, much of the popular history that reaches us does not reflect the actual feelings of the mainstay of the mainstream population—the working people who drove the economy.

What about the Luddites, who felt their jobs and livelihood were so threatened they began smashing the machines in factories? Today, "Luddite" is a term we throw at people who dislike or shun new technology. The original Luddites were skilled British weavers and textile workers, who were afraid that unskilled machine operators were going to make their artisan craft a thing of the past. Kevin Binfield, editor of the collection *Writings of the Luddites,* offers an insightful perspective. He writes that the Luddites "were totally fine with machines." Apparently, they limited their violent attacks to factory owners who wanted to cheat the artisans out of their rightful profits and disregard fair labor practices. "They just wanted machines that made high-quality goods, and they wanted these machines to be run by workers who had gone through an apprenticeship and got paid decent wages. Those were their only concerns."[13]

They called themselves Luddites after Ned Ludd, a young

---

13   Kevin Binfield, ed., Writings of the Luddites, Reprint edition, (Baltimore: Johns Hopkins University Press, 2015)

apprentice who was working at a stocking frame when his boss rapped him for knitting too loosely. According to the story, which may or may not be true, he grabbed a nearby hammer and smashed the machine, shocking both his boss and everyone around him. Word of his trailblazing action reached Nottingham, where the protestors made Ludd their symbolic frontrunner.

In was in Nottingham, in 1811 that the machine smashing first got underway. Other Luddites soon rose up across England, waving sledgehammers about and burning factories. The British government tried to put down the rebels by declaring machine smashing a crime punishable by death. They also sent troops with a generous amount of live ammunition to stop the protests. It was all over within two years.

What resonates with me is a savvy statement in Richard Conniff's article for *Smithsonian Magazine* on "What the Luddites really fought against": "Getting past the myth and seeing their protest more clearly is a reminder that it's possible to live well with technology—but only if we continually question the ways it shapes our lives. It's about small things, like now and then cutting the cord, shutting down the smartphone and going out for a walk."[14]

About now, you've probably noticed a pattern when it comes to the question-asking.

---

14   Richard Conniff, "What the Luddites Really Fought Against," *Smithsonian Magazine*, March 2011, https://www.smithsonianmag.com/history/what-the-luddites-really-fought-against-264412/

The period from the late nineteenth to early twentieth century, also referred to as the Second Industrial Revolution,[15] was also characterized by intense scientific and technological advancements. These brought on dramatic changes in industrial methods, societal structures, and economic markets—which in turn gave birth to the need for new government functions and political diplomacy. From the standpoint of the average western citizen, this was dizzying: telephone, electric light, cinema, radio, bicycle, automobile, airplane. From a scientific and technological standpoint, it was equally revolutionary: anesthetics, public hygiene, sewage, relativity, quantum mechanics, Hubble's astronomy discoveries. Anyone who went to sleep in 1870 and awoke in 1925 would not recognize the world at all!

WAS IT THE SAME FOR THE AGRICULTURAL REVOLUTION?

The Agricultural Revolution, which started in the 1700s, was sparked by the discoveries and advances in science and technology. Farming, along with other industries, was reshaped for efficiency. Land was reallocated and reorganized into compact farms, which meant fewer wasted open fields. Farmers began experimenting with crop rotation and innovative methods to increase the output of their fields, for example, by planting legumes, turnips, and clover. These new crops helped fertilize the fields by improving the earth's

---

15 https://www.britannica.com/topic/history-of-Europe/A-maturing-industrial-society#ref311206

concentration of nitrogen and served as convenient food for the animals. This, in turn, meant farmers could raise more livestock, which introduced more meat for Europeans.

How did the Agricultural Revolution change people's lives? We can sum up the major change as more food for more people.[16] Before the Revolution, people ate what they grew at home. Once agricultural output increased, so did the size of the families. Hunger was a very real problem before the Agricultural Revolution. Many claim the population of England would have starved if not for the Agricultural Revolution, and that the Industrial Revolution may never have taken place.

The new inventions made farming less laborious, more efficient, and cheaper. Again, there were those who felt threatened by these changes. Some farm laborers were concerned that the machines would soon put them out of their jobs. Similar to what happened during the Industrial Revolution, many protested by smashing farm machinery and burning haystacks. The very small percentage of people working on farms today shows they may have been justified over the long term in fearing their jobs would become obsolete. But, at the same time, the mechanization of farms prevented starvation, made the Industrial Revolution possible, and freed these people to train and work in new—and perhaps more rewarding—careers that never existed previously.

---

16 "Agricultural Revolution in England 1500-1850." Mark Overton, BBC, last modified February 17, 2011. http://www.bbc.co.uk/history/british/empire_seapower/agricultural_revolution_01.shtml

POST-WORLD WAR II CHANGES

Over the past decades, Europe has been determined to create a single multicultural identity—it doesn't matter where you come from, you are European. This drive for sameness is whitewashing the importance of heritage and the legacies of different nations and cultures. Does it really make no difference whether I am Portuguese, British, or Lithuanian? How can it be good to erase what makes people special just because some of us are uncomfortable with the difference? Could it be that denying these differences is what's sparking the rise of right-wing conservatism?

Where did this trend start? After World War II, which was seen as having been caused by xenophobia, there was a hefty move to extinguish nationalism and "ensure" there would be no more wars. This is where the seeds to establish the European Union were carefully planted. The drive to create multiculturalism was a strategy to bring about future peace; if we're all the same, there is no reason to fight each other. The plan was to form a peaceful, united, and prosperous Europe within an umbrella political structure in control of domestic affairs, justice standards, security, foreign policy, a common currency, international treaties, and border patrol.

Let's dash through a quick history lesson. Although officially established in 1993, the European Union's foundations go back to 1957, when the European Economic Community (EEC) was established. The EEC was actually formed from the existing European Coal and Steel Community, which started in 1951. In 1993, the Maastricht Treaty was signed, forming the EU. The treaty covered three central aspects: the European Communities, security and foreign policy, and domestic affairs along with standards for justice. In 2009, the Treaty of Lisbon gave the European Union more extensive control, including the authorization to sign international treaties, increased border patrol, and a setup for security and enforcement.

Cut to 2019, and we're now wondering whether trying to eliminate peoples' national identity might be the wrong strategy. It completely ignores our innate human need to feel part of a people and community—to be connected to our roots. For example, nationalism was one of the most heatedly discussed issues in this year's elections for the European Union Parliament. Citizens from over 20 nations headed to the polls to vote whether they prefer populism or closer EU unity. The results came through with a clear message that the traditional parties have lost ground, quite possibly based on fears of a declining Euro and concerns over immigration across the borders. Although the voter turnout was higher than expected, showing that citizens of the EU cared about this governing organization, there was a distinct rise in support for right wing 'identity' parties.

Are we seeing a racist backlash, a rise in nationalism, or both? Nationalism has been an important driver in independence movements like the Irish Revolution or the Zionist movement that created modern Israel. On the flip side, nationalism combined with fascism and a desire for racial unity gave us Nazi Germany. More recently, nationalism was an important impetus for Russia's wrongful annexation of Crimea.

In practice, we can view nationalism as either positive or negative, depending on the context. If you come from a healthy mindset, it is natural to put your own family or people first. The conflict surfaces when we look at our liberal society's attitude toward this natural impulse. Although we're encouraged to "love ourselves" and "put family first," somehow it is not OK to care for your own nation more than other ones.

There's a world of difference between "my people are the most important to me" and "my people are better than any other people." This articulates the distinction between nationalistic patriotism and xenophobia.

Christy Wampole, the author of *Rootedness: The Ramifications of a Metaphor*, cleverly summed this up in her *New York Times* article "Clinging to Our Roots":

> While patriotic nationalism is usually imagined as the polar opposite of diversity-focused multiculturalism, the proponents of each actually have very similar motivations and desires. Each group hopes to preserve or recuperate a sense of rootedness in something. Given the great confusion about how to celebrate one's own roots without insulting someone else's, this struggle will certainly continue in the coming decades.[17]

---

17 Christy Wampole, "Clinging to Our 'Roots,'" The New York Times, May 30, 2016, https://www.nytimes.com/2016/05/30/opinion/clinging-to-our-roots.html

TODAY'S INFORMATION AND COMMUNICATION REVOLUTION

You and I, together with the rest of the modern world, are living through what is being referred to as the Information and Communication Revolution. The development of computers, microchips, the internet, and inexpensive ways to store, visualize, and share information has radically impacted our lives. Beyond the advances themselves, it is the exponential rate of change that has blown everyone away—and is challenging our very ability to adapt.

Think of just a few of the concepts that have infiltrated our lives over the past twenty years: Wi-Fi, smartphones, social media, genetic sequencing, neuroscience, artificial intelligence. It boggles the mind to imagine how much more will change by 2040. Like the previous revolutions we looked at, it is reconditioning how we live, think, interact, prioritize, make decisions, and perceive ourselves.

Let's take a quick look at how we got here. The computer revolution took off in the 1950s, and the internet itself—the big game-changer for many of us—was born in the early 1970s. During the Cold War, the US military and academia needed a system that could guarantee communication would continue between different locations, even if one was nuked or infiltrated. In 1968, this collaboration, known as the Defense Advanced Research Projects Agency (DARPA), demonstrated the first geographically-dispersed network to share information, which then led to the Advanced Research

Projects Agency Network (ARPANET).[18] It was such a hit that soon other large computer sites at universities and government organizations got on board and began linking to the network. This eventually grew into the international network we now call the "internet."

As with other advances, many people in the '50s and '60s were afraid their jobs would be rendered obsolete by computers or robots. Interestingly, while congressmen in the US were holding hearings to reduce unemployment, the US government itself was the biggest advocate of computing technology.[19] They needed computers to run the post office, hold the population census, and forge ahead in the space race. The powerful tech giants colluded with Madison Avenue "madmen," and marketing gurus like Marshall McLuhan, in an effort to calm people's anxieties. They coined terms like "Information Revolution" and "global village," pushing hard to drive the idea that the computer industry was allied with the forces of good.

The internet has come a long way since the days of "Don Draper," especially when we look at the effects social media platforms are having on society. It destroyed previous rules of who owns the information and erased hierarchy in communities and organizations around the world. Alongside blurring the boundaries of what information we can access,

---

18 DARPA, "Arpanet," https://www.darpa.mil/about-us/timeline/arpanet

19 Edmund S. Phelps, "Economic Policy and Unemployment in the 1960s," *National Affairs,* n.d. https://www.nationalaffairs.com/storage/app/uploads/public/58e/1a4/b94/58e1a4b949fa2992935693.pdf

it has radically increased our exposure to different cultures, points of view, and opportunities.

According to a recent report, there were 4.39 billion internet users in 2019, an increase of 366 million (nine percent) versus January 2018.[20] It's not just the number of internet users that is changing. A study by the Pew Research Center found that a large majority of US adults get their news on social media.[21]

With instant access to so much information, and the prevalence of information coming at us from so many social media "influencers," it's tough to get a clear picture of who we are and what we're up against—whether as individuals or communities.

Society is undergoing a fundamental change, as is the definition of the term "community." Community used to mean the people you lived near or the people you were connected to by family ties, geography, or nationality. Today, if you own an adorable Maltese puppy, you have an instant "community" of 12,000 people from around the world waiting to welcome you on Facebook.

Spanish sociologist Manuel Castells examined the societal

---

20   https://wearesocial.com/blog/2019/01/digital-2019-global-internet-use-accelerates

21   Jeffrey Gotfried and Elisa Shearer, "News Use Across Social Media Platforms 2016," *Pew Research Center*, May 26, 2016, https://www.journalism.org/2016/05/26/news-use-across-social-media-platforms-2016

impact of the internet from a global perspective in the MIT Technology Review:

> A primary dimension of these changes is what has been labeled the rise of the Me-centered society, or, in sociological terms, the process of individuation, the decline of community understood in terms of space, work, family, and ascription in general. This is not the end of community, and not the end of place-based interaction, but there is a shift toward the reconstruction of social relationships, including strong cultural and personal ties that could be considered a form of community, on the basis of individual interests, values, and projects.[22]

As Castells notes, if the internet is reforming the definition of communities, it is most certainly revamping the definition of individuals. It's no longer just about people interacting with each other on social media but that social media itself is having a strong influence on our behavior. Think of how often you see friends photographing their dessert in a restaurant or uploading an action photo from their day off. Our behavior itself is changing because of social media. We are taking on different roles, adjusting aspects of our daily routine to get the right angle, trying on different labels, and more.

---

22 Manuel Castells, "The Impact of the Internet on Society: A Global Perspective," *MIT Technology Review*, September 8, 2014, https://www.technologyreview.com/s/530566/the-impact-of-the-internet-on-society-a-global-perspective/

These digital identities present only parts of our lives, and these are shared in a way we would like to be perceived by others—which may or may not be accurate. Where and how does your digital identity diverge from your real one?

Beyond the societal impact on us as individuals, what about the psychological impact? Conflicting research studies continue to report how much social media and screen time is contributing to, or reducing, our stress. Whether good or bad, its impact is undeniable.

Back in 1999, Peter Drucker forecast this in an article for *The Atlantic* titled "Beyond the Information Revolution":

> The psychological impact of the Information Revolution, like that of the Industrial Revolution, has been enormous. It has perhaps been greatest on the way in which young children learn. Beginning at age four (and often earlier), children now rapidly develop computer skills, soon surpassing their elders; computers are their toys and their learning tools.[23]

Today, toddlers from the age of two are being swamped with information and options from the second they open "their" iPad. The sheer number of choices available for sampling can drive anyone over the edge. My eleven-year-old son listens to music on his smartphone, skipping about one-third of the

---

23   Peter Drucker, "Beyond the Information Revolution," *The Atlantic*, October 1999, https://www.theatlantic.com/magazine/archive/1999/10/beyond-the-information-revolution/304658/

way through each song to the next tune. There are simply too many good hits that he doesn't want to miss. Years ago, there would have been ten different activities he could choose to join after school. Today there are over thirty-five after-school programs just within our neighborhood and millions of on-line games and websites. And everything is pushed directly to our devices. You don't even have to search anymore.

LOUD DOES NOT MEAN MANY

As human beings, our main concerns focus on personal security, economic stability, and giving our children the best education possible. This is what is truly important and not related to political ideology or who we are on social media.

Then why is there such a flood of anger, aggressive opinionating, and extreme views on the internet? The eccentric groups and renegade thinkers used to reside outside the norm; they never really got much attention or media focus. Today, if they shout loud enough, we hear their voices over the internet—and it will inevitably sound like they've got a substantial following. Thankfully, they represent the loud, not the many.

YouTube recently started labeling this type of extremist material as "borderline content." Worse still, this type of content tends to go viral among those hanging out on the social periphery, consuming misinformation, conspiracy theories, and the like. Then it's picked up by news stations, promoted through late-night comedy shows, and circulated as memes—all the while drawing even more followers. Years ago, there was no way the concept of the earth being flat would have come up in any of our conversations.

Perhaps, like me, you see yourself as a moderate and modern thinker. I was taught that there is no need to shout or to state the obvious. But today it's essential to make our voices heard. We can't allow the only loud voices to be those of political extremists, people who believe the earth is flat, conspiracy theorists, or Holocaust deniers—all of whom ultimately gather momentum through their loud shouting. We might drive the economy, but we don't speak up.

Perhaps you are asking, "What is there to shout about? I just want to quietly live my life and not feel uneasy about the changes going on 'out there.'" Many of us face this dilemma—when is it good to speak up, when is it too assertive, and when is it appropriate to state our opinions and challenge colleagues? Here too, the range of our comfort zone is what keeps us from speaking our piece. The good news is that you can actively expand this zone so you can speak up for what you believe in and not fear being "punished" for stating your opinion. If you firmly believe that you have a right to speak out, even a duty to speak out, then you will have the confidence to do so. Giving someone else your perspective by stating facts or asking simple questions is an elegant but effective way to make your point. Take a stand, believe in your own statements, and step out of your comfort zone to confront those extremists who challenge common sense with their theories of conspiracy and victimization.

LEAVING BEHIND THE BLAME GAME

When you complain, you make yourself into a victim. When you speak out, you are in your power. So change the situation by taking action or by speaking out if necessary or possible; leave the situation or accept it. All else is madness.

— **Eckhart Tolle**

One common trend among these loud voices is that something is very wrong with the world and it's the fault of some group, cause, or organization. The underlying theme is one of frustration. Of course, it's convenient to have someone else feed you news, views, and opinions on social media. The problem is, they are neither presenting you with information and options nor letting you form your own opinion.

Open any news site and you will see headlines proclaiming that the world is in chaos, along with who is at fault–whether it's your local government, senior politicians and their Twitter accounts, the industrialists and their energy-hungry machines, the meat-eaters and their contribution to global warming, the religious extremists, or the Israelis. The moment someone else feeds you your opinion, you are no longer in charge.

Don't get me wrong, it's right to be vigilant, raise awareness, and call out hateful ideologies. But deep down inside you know that, in the long run, the blame game leads nowhere. Although the short term feeling of having someone to blame might give you a lift, this thought direction means someone else is in control—you are powerless and you're the victim. That's when the world gets even more uncomfortable and frustrating.

Take the Flat Earth Society as an example. How can 214,000 people believe the earth is flat?[24] We just talked about Copernicus shaking the foundations of society, yet 500 years later we have hundreds of thousands ready to ignore proven scientific facts! An average, intelligent person would look to NASA authorities or research and seek the "truth." The mantra of these and other outliers is to blame the intellectuals for conspiring to fool people—it's not about asking questions, sharing knowledge, discovering facts, and looking into history. Why would someone join the Flat Earth Society? They want to belong. It's not an intellectual choice based on information. It's a choice to be a victim of the conspiracy that is planting fake evidence about the world being round (and the moon landing of course) and trying to "pull the wool over your eyes."

Everyone has moments in their life when they feel that someone has wronged them. As long as this is a temporary space in your day, you're right in line with natural human tendencies. When it becomes your life motto and shapes your outlook into that of a victim, you are no longer taking responsibility. The problem will remain until someone else changes something.

---

24 Taken from Facebook, July2019. https://www.facebook.com/pg/
    FlatEarthToday/community/?ref=page_internal

It's infinitely more appealing to believe that you are not a loser; things are not going well because some immigrant took your job, Wall Street took your money, or your parents didn't give you enough.

No one else can, or should, be responsible for your destiny or contentment. Once you take responsibility for where you are and the decisions you make, you stop being a victim. You are in charge. You don't feel threatened by other people, different opinions, new definitions, trends in society, or opportunities. Your mind is open to the new.

Taking it one step further, you can't truly be liberal and accepting unless you know who you are and feel comfortable with the differences between you and others— you cannot ignore these differences. This is part of the problem with some people who call themselves liberals, who react aggressively or even violently when leaders relate to other people's different needs or the need for policies regarding these differences. You can live peacefully with others if you accept each other, together with accepting the differences.

A few weeks ago, I met an Arab woman in front of the Museum of the Jewish People. She understood that I was in a position of responsibility and expressed her outrage that the museum covered only the Jewish people. I said, "I would be happy to do the same for your people. Every nation should have its story told in a way that gets its people emotionally invested and encourages them to connect to their roots." The museum is a good model of how to build an open, welcoming environment in which anyone can feel comfortable learning about their people and draw strength. One museum does not diminish the heritage of another people.

Judging others happens when you feel overprotective of who you are—and this is hard to do when you are protecting a vacuum. An example of this is the overreaction of countries across Europe to the Muslim dress codes for women. Many debate the need to limit or allow various forms of the body covering hijab and the niqab, which covers the entire face except for the eyes. The debate covers many issues from religious freedom to female equality and goes on from there to terrorism and multiculturalism in Europe. How do you know when a woman wants or needs to be liberated? If you find yourself reacting emotionally to the rights of others, try to stop and understand why it disturbs you so deeply. Then you can make the right choice about what is right for you and where you want to direct your energy.

I wrote about blame and victimhood back in 2017, in an article for *The Jerusalem Post*,[25] and why we shouldn't let these feelings restrict our realm of possibilities. When we feel we have been wronged, we want to figure out who is to blame. I described it as a tiny injection of moral righteousness that gives you a temporary high, a friend who never lets you down.

25 Irina Nevzlin, "A Collective Rosh Hashana Experiment," *The Jerusalem Post*, September 19, 2017, https://www.jpost.com/Opinion/A-collective-Rosh-Hashana-experiment-505543

The difference between being a victim and assuming responsibility for your life, and therefore being a free person, is a matter of choice. The more we opt for responsibility and the less we choose the victim narrative and strategy, the more leverage we will have over our lives to move forward and enjoy pursuing new directions.

This brings me back to my years growing up as a minority. Immigrants don't have the luxury of blaming anyone for where they live, their lack of a job, absence of friends, or shoddy apartment. They made the choice to move and now it is up to them to build a new life and make it successful. Most have no expectations about someone else helping them and therefore no feelings of victimhood.

I am by no means denying the fact that life has its share of difficulties and tragedies. Many of us have experienced or witnessed social injustices based on race, gender, or physical characteristics. My point is that, although you cannot control the behavior or discriminatory actions of others, you can decide whether you see yourself as a victim of these people or as the person in charge of your own life. True, certain directions may be blocked by other people but that does not give them control over your ability to thrive and succeed. Your attitude going forward is up to you. Do you remain stuck and frustrated or do you continue advancing nonetheless because you are the one who makes the decisions?

Like minorities, you need to make a conscious choice not to be a victim. By conscious I mean sitting down with yourself and engaging in a serious dialog about who you are as an individual and along what trajectories you would like to move. You can choose to be radically free and to open up an infinite realm of new and unexpected possibilities.

* Not having a tribe, ~~the~~ anymore, feel + alienated -

Biologically, we are meant to be in connection. BA Industrial Revolution - we were on the same farm, around same people.

CHAPTER 3

Why immigrants can help us find a solution

Between 1980 and 2015, the worldwide population of migrants more than doubled to a total of 231,522,000.[26] Once these intrepid people decide to move to a new country, they have to navigate new cultures and identities, yet they somehow manage to feel at home in a place where the old and familiar is no longer relevant. The processes they go through, the flexibility demanded of them, and the way they deal with the new, makes them an ideal role model. Like them, we face the challenges of adapting daily to new paradigms and attitudes.

Many people make the mistake of viewing immigrant newcomers as people with few resources and a slim chance of thriving. This false narrative has them scraping the bottom of the barrel when it comes to opportunity and success, but it is simply not true. Let's take a closer look at people who made a conscious choice, for whatever reason, to leave their

---

26   Migr. Policy Inst. Data Hub. 2014. http://migrationpolicy.org/programs/data-hub

country of residence and move to a new home. You'll see why immigrants and minorities—even more than majority populations—have the characteristics and mindset that makes them better equipped and more capable of having a meaningful life in the midst of changing times.

I like to think of this type of immigrant newcomer as a "rooted cosmopolitan." In the 1940s, around the same time that Maslow published his epic paper on the human hierarchy of needs, Stalin coined a derogatory term for Jews, calling them "rootless cosmopolitans." This was basically an anti-Semitic label and campaign to put down people who supposedly were not loyal to the Soviet regime. As we know, the country you live in physically is just that—where you live. The people and culture you come from are your real roots. Like the tree metaphor, staying rooted is what keeps us strong in a vast and open world when confusion reigns.

Unlike the majority, immigrants have no choice but to be strong and make it on their own

When you are a minority in a new country you lack many resources that are already in place for the majority. Immigrants generally arrive with no connections, fewer economic resources, and sometimes not a word of the language spoken. If you are a Ukrainian newly arrived in Argentina, you'll find yourself in an environment that does not celebrate your holidays, won't love your food, doesn't speak your language, and is generally low on everything you find comforting and familiar. You are in a state of not-knowing and not-having.

And you probably knew this would be the case before you arrived in Argentina. The prevalent coping mechanism for immigrants is their determined attitude: I have to work harder to bring myself and my family to the level that this society lives in because I have no other choice.

This brings me to the first set of skills that minorities possess and majorities sometimes lack—accepting full responsibility for your own life and what you make of it. As a native Brit born in the majority, you might be the third generation of your family studying at Oxford. Even if you lack talent and skills, your parents might have a connection that can open the door to a decent job. When you've lived somewhere your whole life, you have family, school buddies, neighbors, colleagues, and friends of friends. You have contacts, a flag, a passport, and a sense of (false?) confidence. In short, you have people to lean on—and they can help you succeed.

Many immigrant parents throughout the ages have told their children that they must be twice as good and work twice as hard as anyone else because they start from nothing and it is up to them to shape their destiny.

Unlike the majority, you need to establish a feeling of being at home in your new country. To accomplish this, you invest more energy in being with your own kind—whether it's around food, traditions, or holidays. It's a common mistake to look at this solidarity and "stickiness" between immigrants as something that makes a minority weaker. What these communities are actually doing is making themselves stronger by uniting and connecting to their shared heritage. We've all seen how minorities tend to live in "ghettos." If I'm an Italian immigrant in San Francisco, I might have a job at the bank, but I'll come back to the neighborhood Italian restaurant for dinner, perhaps go to church, and make an effort to maintain close-knit ties with family. This keeps me connected to my roots.

Another skill that immigrants naturally strengthen is decision-making. Building a new life involves an enormous amount of decisions, all the time, every day, over and over again. As anyone who has ever moved to a new apartment or done renovations knows, making decisions and culling the different options can be exhausting—to the point that many people give up midstream. Yes, that's how we end up with the naked light bulbs in the hallway ceiling when everything else is done up so nicely. Even immigrants who come from a privileged background have to deal with adapting to a brand new culture on an ongoing basis. They're forced to re-think and examine each and every thing, from clothes and food to social norms and which careers are worthwhile.

STEPPING OUT OF AUTOPILOT

We have so many things in life that we do without even thinking. We get out of bed, brush our teeth, have breakfast, go to work, see the same people, eat the same foods. We live on autopilot much of our lives. Immigrants can't and don't. Even when it comes to these simple everyday tasks, the toothbrush is now different, the cheese is not the same as back home, and navigating the roads is a whole new challenge.

Being an immigrant is a type of reawakening—very similar to what we are going through in this new era of change. When you live outside your comfort zone, you simply don't have the luxury of living on standby. Being in a new country automatically triggers the need to be fully present and much more alert.

Learning to "be present" is one of the most essential skills you can nurture to have a fulfilling life. It involves slowing down and observing what is going on around you. It means acknowledging what exists in your life and accepting that you have to take charge over how you interact with different (and quite often strange) aspects of your surroundings. It involves making decisions that are based on real needs, thereby creating a personal identity that is flexible and long-lasting. This is the key to instilling more serenity and flexibility into your mindset.

ADAPTING TO NEW CULTURAL NORMS

Immigrants know what it feels like to be an outsider. Their names, accent, appearance, and mannerisms all mark them as different. These too are aspects that lead to questions: Do I change my name? Do I work on losing my accent? Do I want to hang on to my unique style or blend in? Who makes up my circle of friends?

Some immigrants start out hoping they can stay pretty much the same as they are and just seek out others with comparable values, experiences, and cultural norms. This is a very natural "energy-saving" strategy. But if there is a big enough community of people from the same homeland, they run the risk of remaining stagnant and not exploring what lies beyond their in-group. That's one extreme.

The other extreme lies in overcompensating and completely disassociating from their previous culture. "I'm going to be more British than James Bond." Ultimately, everyone has to begin forming their new identity—by questioning and exploring what works and what doesn't. This identity will be one that balances the new and fascinating with the old and familiar. Sometimes a person can go too far in endorsing the new or abandoning the old, but eventually the pendulum settles in a stable balance. When you are ready to ignite this process of questioning and exploration, rest assured that you will still be you—perhaps even more so—even when the pendulum is swinging.

When I moved to England, I faced similar tough issues. I had to take stock of what I came with as a person, note the new ideas and information coming at me, and decide what I needed to adopt. I initially assumed I had a decent advantage where language was concerned because I already spoke English—or thought I did. I had studied English and worked at an American company in Russia. But when my new life in London got underway, I had trouble understanding what my colleagues at work were saying. I'd go out shopping and couldn't grasp what people were talking about. I had no choice. It was time to start reading newspapers, watching TV, signing up for online courses, and bravely asking people to speak more slowly.

Then there was the food. I was raised on a combination of Jewish-Russian food—we're talking root vegetables, lots of carbs, with pepper and salt for flavoring. Moving to a new country opened my eyes to a whole collection of culinary delights. Do I like fish and chips or shepherd's pie? And who knew you could enjoy an upscale dining experience on the second floor of a gastropub?

At the supermarket, nothing was familiar. Which carton held regular milk? What kind of bread is similar to the one I liked back home and which new one should I try? Even a simple outing to get basic staples for breakfast required a good dollop of decision-making, exploration, and adaptation. I had to step out of my comfort zone every day—whether it was shopping, interacting with people, voicing my opinion in the office, or navigating the transportation. The first time I got behind the wheel and had to drive "on the wrong side of the road," I ended up crashing right into a double-decker bus. This really "drove home" how we automatically revert to the paradigms our brain is used to, even when they are no longer valid.

Adapting to new ways of thinking and doing will exercise a different part of your brain. When you live in a new place, you don't have the option of letting that "muscle" go slack.

Years ago, the prevailing theory was that our gray matter does not change drastically after childhood.[27] More recently, scientists studying the brains of animals found that those who lived in a changing environment—with new toys that prompted learning new tasks—had more developed brains than those who lived in a static environment. Closer examination of the animals' brains showed that the "busy and challenged" animals had more connections between nerve cells in their brains. Their neural connections were also stronger and more substantial, resulting in an amazing ten percent growth in the mass of the brain itself. Other research studies even went as far as demonstrating the growth of new neural cells in the hippocampus of mice and other animals that lived in an enriched environment that demanded continuous learning. These animals also proved to be better at solving problems and learning than the ones who lived a sedate life. It is no surprise that later research with humans demonstrated that learning new tasks is critical for the brain's structure.

This strengthening of brain "muscles" had its parallel metaphor when I began having problems with my voice. I was getting hoarse and quickly made an appointment with a speech therapist. She said, "You speak more quietly and at a lower volume than what your vocal cords need." Apparently, the muscle had atrophied; it needed to be challenged to get stronger. Imagine being told as an adult that you need to learn how to speak properly!

---

27   Joenna Driemeyer et al., "Changes in Gray Matter Induced by Learning – Revisited," *PLOS ONE*, (July 23, 2008), https://journals.plos.org/plosone/article?id=10.1371/journal.pone.0002669

Hard to get in new habits — like brain muscle.

To embrace change, you need an open "beginner's mind" that is willing to be trained. The beginner's mind has no expectations or preconceived ideas. When you move to a new country, you don't have any choice but to see everything with fresh eyes and move into training mode. Of course, that doesn't mean you can only strengthen this muscle if you move to a new country. But we'll get to that in a later section.

Learning a new language is another essential skill that immigrants must engage in. Being able to interact with people and the new environment is a matter of survival. Going beyond the basic translation of words, immigrants have to learn common phrases, humor, cultural signposts, historical references…all of it a new world to be explored.

Friendships—both existing and new ones—are another layer of culture that immigrants end up re-evaluating. Often, your friends are your friends because they've always been there. Having friends from childhood is a gift, and this is something immigrants don't have. But you probably have some friends who you would rather not spend much time with. Do you keep these friendships going because you don't want to hurt them, because they may badmouth you if you drop them, or because they're next-door neighbors with your great-uncle? There are many reasons we keep friends who no longer contribute positive energy to our lives.

When you move to a new country, your old friendships are all on the line. At first, you reach out by calling them, chatting on Skype, or staying glued to Facebook. Then an interesting thing happens, you no longer have the time. Those people who are truly important are the ones with whom you stay in touch. And then something really fascinating happens, you make friends as a grown-up in your new culture. This whole process cultivates your ability to get closure and discontinue relationships that are no longer fulfilling. It also trains you to open up and trust new people. As an immigrant, you simply do not have the option of skipping over this process.

WHAT MAKES A SUCCESSFUL IMMIGRANT?

Immigrants are known for having an intense pride in anyone successful who shares their heritage. If a celebrity, success-ful author, or popular politician is of immigrant origin, all members of that community claim him or her as their own. But the statistics go beyond pride. For example, Nigerians are better educated than native-born Americans.[28] Jews make up less than 0.2 percent of the global population but twenty percent of the Nobel Prize winners.[29] And the success of immigrant entrepreneurs is known to be proportionately higher than for native-born individuals. The numbers show this to be true both in the United States, where immigrants

---

28 Spencer Critchley, "African Immigrants are Better Educated than Americans," *Huffpost*, December 1, 2018, https://www.huffpost.com/entry/african-immigrants-are-better-educated-than-ameri-cans_b_5a58f7cde4b01ccdd48b5bcb

29 Nataly Kelly, "Research Shows Immigrants Help Businesses Grow. Here's Why," *Harvard Business Review*, October 26, 2018, https://hbr.org/2018/10/research-shows-immigrants-help-businesses-grow-heres-why

make up close to thirty percent of all entrepreneurs but only thirteen percent of the general population, and in other countries.[30]

A Harvard Business school study by Sari Pekkala Kerr and William Kerr compared the businesses founded by immigrants to those founded by native-born citizens.[31] Apparently, immigrant-led companies grow more quickly and are more likely to survive long term. According to *Quartz* magazine, 216 companies on the Fortune 500 were founded by immigrants or their children.[32] We don't have to look far to find examples like Warner Brothers, Intel, Google, eBay, Estee Lauder, and Levi's. When asked about the reason for this success, William Kerr noted, "The very act of someone moving around the world, often leaving family behind, might select those who are very determined or more tolerant of business risk."

Nataly Kelly agrees with this statement in her *Harvard*

30   Robert W. Fairlie et al., *Startup Activity: National Trends*, (Kansas City: Ewing Marion Kauffman Foundation, 2016), https://www. kauffman.org/~/media/kauffman_org/microsites/kauffman_index/ startup_activity_2016/kauffman_index_startup_activity_national_trends_2016.pdf

31   Sari Pekkala Kerr and William R. Kerr, "Immigrant Entrepreneurship." *NBER Working Paper No. 22385*, July 2016, http://www.nber. org/papers/w22385

32   Ana Campoy, "216 Companies on the Fortune 500 were Founded by Immigrants or their Children," *Quartz*, December 9, 2017, https:// qz.com/1151689/216-companies-on-the-fortune-500-were-founded-by-immigrants-or-their-children/

Business Review article of 2018:

> People who are willing to uproot their lives in search of something better are the types of people who are determined to make change happen themselves. To migrate to a new country also takes a high level of confidence in one's ability to change and a high level of tolerance for uncertainty. More importantly, they believe in their ability to figure things out and adapt once they get there.[33]

In short, immigrants prove the immense value of facing new challenges and exploring uncharted territory.

The numbers don't really come as a surprise. After all, the US was built by immigrants and it makes sense that it has retained that entrepreneurial spirit. As opposed to the Soviet Union, where a single national identity was enforced instead of enabling ethnic pluralism to flourish, US citizens were never deprived of their roots. Although the country faces its fair share of racism, most Americans share a national identity that exists in harmony with tribal or ethnic identities. In fact, individuals from various subgroups often feel a strong common identity with and loyalty to the larger American community.

Of course, not all immigrants were created equal and not

---

33 Nataly Kelly, "Research Shows Immigrants Help Businesses Grow. Here's Why." *Harvard Business Review* article of 10/2018

all experience success in their host countries. Many pundits consider Muslim immigration to France to be a dismal failure. Muslim immigrants began arriving forty years ago and have still not been successfully integrated as a people, although there are many eminent individuals. And why are so many Indians and Pakistanis still struggling in Britain, while others serve as executives in large multinational corporations? What we do know is that anyone who immigrates possesses no small amount of courage. Transplanting yourself is a risky process and not everyone will succeed. But the fact that immigrants are newcomers does mean they are forced to develop skills that make them more adaptable and flexible—ready to face a world that is changing and open.

Stephen Dubner of Freakonomics fame hosted a podcast examining the success of Lebanese immigrants. To date, more than half of the Lebanese people reside outside the country and are generally considered to be highly influential. Is it a factor of genetics? Or maybe the immigrant network that allows a person to call up any Lebanese in any city and ask for help? As part of the interview, Lebanese author Nassim Taleb talked about the mass emigrations that resulted from the crash of the silk market in the nineteenth century and the brutal civil war in 1975. He is convinced that: "…it is this volatility that has helped make Lebanese emigres so successful."[34] His theory is not all that different from what was noted

---

34 Stephen Dubner, "Who are the Most Successful Immigrants in the World?" *Freakonomics*, Episode 137. Podcast audio, August 2013, http://freakonomics.com/podcast/who-are-the-most-successful-immigrants-in-the-world/

earlier: biological systems react better to stressors.

A touch of adversity is likely to make you stronger because you suddenly have to pay attention to what you're doing. You can no longer function on autopilot and keep doing the usual. Just for the record, here are a few of the famous people with Lebanese heritage: designer Eli Saab, actors Selma Hayek and Danny Thomas, music stars Shakira and Casey Kasem, even Manuel Moroun who owns the bridge between Canada and Detroit.

WHAT CAN IMMIGRANT TEENS TEACH US?

Fascinating research by Andrew Fuligni and Kim Tasi points to adolescents from immigrant families as champions of flexibility when it comes to social and cultural changes. According to their study: "adolescents from immigrant families often demonstrate levels of psychological, behavioral, and educational adjustment that are either equal to or even greater than those of their peers from native-born families."[35] Although these teens grow up well-entrenched in their host society, their personal identity is closely associated with their native cultural values. In short, they remain connected to their roots.

Remarkably, these teens have an innate understanding that

---

35   Adolescents Andrew J. Fuligni and Kim M. Tsai, "Developmental Flexibility in the Age of Globalization: Autonomy and Identity Development Among Immigrant Adolescents," *Annual Review of Psychology*, 66, (2015).

they can, and must, pick and choose from both the old and new cultural norms as they build their personal identities. Will the daughter of a Chinese immigrant to the US identity herself as Chinese, Asian, or American—or all three? According to the research, adolescents create a new hybrid identity that combines different values and attitudes from their immigrant families and host country. It is exactly this flexibility that gives them an advantage over their native peers when it comes to adjusting to new situations.

The social, cultural, and economic changes faced by these adolescents force them to find creative ways to express their identity and independence while remaining connected to their roots. When it comes to changes posed by today's Information and Communication Revolution, the authors firmly believe that: "The many patterns of identity and autonomy development that have been observed among immigrants foreshadow the future experiences of many of those who stay in their native countries.[36]"

WHY CONNECTING TO YOUR ROOTS IS THE PLACE TO START

The nation, of course, is still a meaningful unit. For centuries, people have died, and continue to die, for their nations. No one, on the other hand, will ever be willing to die for "global," as a friend of mine wisely put it. In fact, globalism seems to challenge the very

---

36   ibid

possibility of rootedness, at least the kind that once re-lied on nation-states for its symbolic power. How will people be rooted in the future if global networks replace nations? Through bloodlines? Ideologies? Shared cultural practices? Elective affinities? Will we become comfortable rooting ourselves in rootlessness?

— **Christy Wampole**[37]

Being rooted—cultivating your tradition, culture, and history—is a solid place to start when it comes to dealing with a difficult and perplexing world. Your people or tribe is a support group whose members have a sense of shared responsibility. These social groups give us an anchor when everything else is in flux. Of course, if you are only concerned about your own people or nation, you can end up being overly rooted and isolated from the world at large.

The ideal solution is to be rooted and open.

In the past, especially during the eighteenth-century Enlightenment, cosmopolites or "citizens of the world" took pains to learn about and share knowledge regarding their roots. As "rooted cosmopolitans," we too can take pride in understanding our traditions and our place within them. If you are educated about your roots and know who you are, you already have a secure point of reference for venturing forth. Unlike the loud angry extremists, you will not see

---

37 Christy Wampole, "Clinging to our roots" *New York Times* article 05/2016

yourself as a victim or feel intimidated by different customs, ideas, and beliefs.

This is personified in the universal message of the Dalai Lama, who has inspired so many people to search for happiness. He travels the world, meeting with crowds and diplomats, yet goes to sleep every night at 9:30. He doesn't feel the need to adapt to anyone else's schedule or customs. He maintains a strong connection to his Tibetan roots, way of life, and manner of dress—yet millions of people relate to his message and flock to hear his words.

Deepening the connection with your roots is one of the most essential things you can do to begin enjoying life. It's yours, and no one can take it.

What if you have been blessed with a mixed bag of ethnic roots? Perhaps this makes it even more imperative to research and learn about the different aspects of your heritage and see for yourself the different roles these assets can play in your life.

Where do you begin? Start by asking questions.

Most of us are happy to talk about ourselves and spend a good deal of the time thinking about "me." After all, we are the main characters in our personal stories. But, if you think about it, having a conversation with your grandmother or distant cousin is really about you. When you ask how she went through the war, you are not doing her a favor—it will enrich and strengthen you as an individual. Visit old relatives, ask about their lives, and you will begin to see your own life from a different perspective.

How is this different from speaking to your immigrant colleague at the fitness club? With an acquaintance, it's about information—their people, their profession, their lifestyle. When it's your grandparent, it's about you. The fitness coach may inform you or amuse you; this nourishes the leaves of your tree but not the roots.

The eminent Samuel Huntington did a brilliant job of summing this up in his book *The Clash of Civilizations*:

> In the post–Cold War world, the most important distinctions among peoples are not ideological, political, or economic. They are cultural. Peoples and nations are attempting to answer the most basic question humans can face: Who are we? And they are answering that question in the traditional way human beings have answered it, by reference to the things that mean most to them. People define themselves in terms of ancestry, religion, language, history, values, customs, and institutions. They identify with cultural groups: tribes, ethnic groups, religious communities, nations, and, at the broadest level, civilizations.[38]

---

38 Huntington, Samuel *The Clash of Civilizations and the Remaking of World Order* (NY: Simon and Schuster Paperbacks, 2011)

EVERYONE HAS ROOTS

You were born somewhere and to someone. You have parents, places, languages, and cultures in your history—whether you know about it or not. Understanding what and who you come from is critical—whether you connect with it or decide that you can't relate to the entire package. It's a part of who you are.

At this point, you might ask: Why not channel my efforts into erasing my roots, alongside old non-relevant values, and start from a clean slate? Why not continuously examine other new ideas, values, cultures, foods, types of music, or beliefs to try them out—and then build my own blend of traditions? Wouldn't this be where we really give everything encountered a fair chance, where every single thing is questioned?

I am all for questioning everything and discovering new ideas. But ignoring the basis of your own identity and trying on everyone else's would be like going into a major department store and trying on every single item of clothing. And it could take a lifetime. Clearly, this wouldn't be an efficient use of your energy, especially when there is a section in the store that has the item you're looking for and in your size. You might not like everything that is on offer, but doesn't it make more sense to start your search in an area tailored to you? Once you start looking through the "merchandise," you will either find some answers, or not. Sometimes you will just end up thinking about what you saw, and sometimes searching through your roots will be a fascinating way to strengthen your "muscle" for exploration and adventure.

As gracefully pointed out by Douglas Murray in *The Strange Death of Europe: Immigration, Identity, Islam*:

> We know that the Greeks today are not the same people as the Ancient Greeks. We know that the English are not the same today as they were a millennium ago, nor the French the French. And yet they are recognizably Greek, English and French and all are European. In these and other identities we recognize a degree of cultural succession: a tradition that remains with certain qualities (positive as well as negative), customs and behaviors. We recognize the great movements of the Normans, Franks and Gauls brought about great changes. And we know from history that some movements affect a culture relatively little in the long term whereas others can change it irrevocably. The problem comes not with an acceptance of change, but with the knowledge that when those changes come too fast or are too different we become something else—including something we may never have wanted to be.[39]

Speaking of Greeks, on a recent trip to Athens with my son, I couldn't help but see the delightful neighborhood of Anafiotika as a perfect example of people preserving their roots—both physically and metaphorically. In the

---

39 Douglas Murray, *The Strange Death of Europe: Immigration, Identity, Islam*, (London: Bloomsbury, 2017).

mid-nineteenth century, when Athens became a capital, expert builders had to be imported to refurbish the royal palace for the first Greek king, King Otto. Most of these workers came from the Greek island of Anafi and other Cycladic islands—hence the name Anafiotika for the quarter where they lived in Athens. During the day, they would labor for the king, building in a neo-classical style. But at night, they returned to an area that reminded them of the homes they missed. Their neighborhood embodied the Cycladic architecture style with small white cubicle houses, bougainvillea, and blue roofs that make way for a view of the sea. To this day, the tiny neighborhood inside Athens is still one of the most picturesque areas to preserve authentic Greek island charm.

The deeper you connect to your family history and roots, the stronger your foundation as a person. Making this connection is different for every one of us. You can connect to your roots through family, genealogy, food, geography, religion, literature, music, architecture—whatever makes you feel that you're at home and understand yourself better. It involves both knowing and connecting—one with your brain and one with your heart.

CHAPTER 4

Some ideas on getting to know who you are

"Be yourself; everyone else is already taken"

— Oscar Wilde

We looked at newcomer immigrants and how they build resilience. Of course, you don't have to move countries to adopt this mindset and spark new ways of thinking. This chapter touches on a few fundamental guidelines that can help you start seeing things from a different perspective. You can easily find resources that go into further detail on these and other ways to deal with the discomfort of facing the new and complex.

You can lighten feelings of agitation and anxiety in the changing world by having a solid grasp of who you are. It's a firm base to stand on while you filter all the new information and opinions coming at you. This way, when you learn to ask who you are, and what works for you, you won't have a problem exploring, examining, accepting or rejecting the new.

First, I will share some strategies that can help break down and simplify the process of getting to know your inner self. Next, we'll look at the importance of learning about your roots and feeling a sense of collective identity and belonging. After that, you should be ready to explore some basic skills that can help you transition to the continuous practice of asking what is right for you, thinking critically, and thinking ahead.

SHAPING YOUR LIFE

"In the long run, we shape our lives, and we shape ourselves. The process never ends until we die. And the choices we make are ultimately our own responsibility."

— **Eleanor Roosevelt**

EMBRACING CHANGE AS AN OPPORTUNITY

There are many theories about why we often feel so uncomfortable with change. A few of these are summed up by Tobore Onojighofia in his work *On Energy Efficiency and the Brain's Resistance to Change.*[40] The idea of resistance to change has been a central topic of interest since the early days of social psychology. As humans, we instinctively avoid any departure from the ways we're used to doing things. Because our brain uses about twenty percent of our body's

---

40 Tobore Onojighofia, *On Energy Efficiency and the Brain's Resistance to Change: The Neurological Evolution of Dogmatism and Close-Mindedness*, (Baltimore: Johns Hopkins University Bloomberg School of Public Health, 2018).

energy requirement, it makes sense that a good brain would come up with smart ways to do less work. And doing things the same way you always did them saves on brainpower.[41] A number of studies suggest that the brain builds its own internal models of "how the world works." This helps it conserve energy so we don't have to continuously expend effort relearning what we already know. This same ability helps us remember important objects or people, what aspect of our life they fit into, where they are located, and how they affect us. On the other hand, this same energy-saving phenomenon makes our brain resist the new.[42]

The same holds true for the beliefs and paradigms that have been around for decades. People naturally gravitate toward and remember information that is in line with their pre-existing views. When it comes to survival, this makes it easier for us to predict and prepare for what's coming up, and to make decisions on what to do—either before it happens or when it happens. Our brain likes order and structure. What's more, we are likely to feel at ease with new situations if someone we trust or see as an expert thinks they are positive. Makes sense, right?

This inherent desire for comfort, stability, and sameness, means the term "change" arouses a lot of emotions, both positive and negative. We sense both excitement and fear;

41   J.M. Kinney and H.N. Tucker, eds., *Energy Metabolism: Tissue Determinants and Cellular Corollaries*, (New York: Raven, 1992).

42   Onojighofia, *On Energy Efficiency*

but really, all of life is change. It's a process and a journey that brings us new things every day. Most of us would cringe at the thought of knowing in advance exactly what every day will have in store for us. So why not embrace these new opportunities?

Resilience is the most accurate term for this ability to embrace change and respond by either taking action or simply "flowing with it"—as opposed to struggling against it. By learning to be more resilient, you can dissipate the panic and feel more comfortable with all the "craziness" of today. I'm very much in tune with Daniel Goleman's optimistic perspective: "...there's an increasing body of empirical evidence showing that resilience—whether in children, survivors of concentration camps, or businesses back from the brink—can be learned."[43] He notes that most resilience theories discuss three common characteristics shared by resilient people: a strong acceptance of reality, a deep belief that life is meaningful, and an uncanny ability to improvise and bounce back.

Discomfort about change comes from the uncertainty of what's coming up and what the situation will require from you. It's all about gaps in information and your immediate reaction to what you don't know, what you can't possibly know, and how the information you don't know will affect you. The best way to counter this is to see it as an

43   Daniel Goleman et al., *Resilience*, HBR Emotional Intelligence Series, (Cambridge: Harvard Business Review Press, 2017).

opportunity to discover something new. That's right—slow down, and before reacting or over-reacting, ask questions and start looking for information. What is making me un-comfortable? What do I have control over and what is out of my hands? Can I learn a new skill or gain knowledge to deal more elegantly with the situation? If I do something differently or don't do something, how will it influence the way I feel or my well-being? You will always come out of this process feeling calmer and smarter.

DEVELOPING INTERNAL BOUNDARIES

Knowing who you are means knowing your internal versus external boundaries. For me, the first time I put limits on my children's behavior for my own well-being and not their safety or education, was a lesson in resilience. I had returned home from a harrowing day of meetings and I needed to regroup my thoughts—or maybe just relax a bit. But more importantly, I needed the children to chill out and end their day—for me. Yes, it was about me. This was a new thought: my well-being matters, not just theirs. I gathered the boys and explained that, "This noise level is not working for me. I need to sleep now and you can't stay up." I recognized and shared with them my own internal boundary. At first, they resisted because it was a change, but then they got with the program. Reflecting and then taking fresh action in a new situation can empower you as a parent. Then you can use this approach for bigger issues where you put yourself first—of course, not at the expense of someone else's health or safety. My friend has a saying for this: "You decide—the world will adjust. And so it does."

DISCOVERING YOUR PERSONAL IDENTITY VERSUS HAVING IT HANDED TO YOU

"Let go of who you think you're supposed to be; embrace who you are."

— Brené Brown

During our teenage years, many of us faced fundamental questions of identity within our families and communities: Who am I? Where do I belong? What decisions can I make for myself and when am I bound to do what others dictate—whether it comes from parents, a boss, friends, or sports coach? Although authorities such as Erikson note the importance of these questions in identity formation during adolescence, these are the same basic questions of identity that we must continue to ask throughout life.[44] Sociologist James E. Cote noted that if these questions are ignored or not answered successfully, problems can arise when it comes to identity formation.[45]

Is identity something you have, something you build, or something to be acquired? What does the term identity really encompass?

For me, identity is a process and not an end result. The

---

44   E. Erikson, *Identity: Youth and Crisis*, (New York: Norton, 1968).

45   J.E. Cote, "Identity formation and self-development in adolescence," In *Handbook of Adolescent Psychology*, R.M. Lerner and L. Steinberg, eds., pp. 266–304, (New York: Wiley, 2009).

nicely: "People with strong self-awareness are neither overly critical nor unrealistically hopeful. Rather, they are honest—with themselves and with others."[46]

This inner voice was squashed by generations being taught as children exactly how to act politely, but with little attention paid to how we feel and what is going on inside us. We are told to behave properly and say things that will make others feel at ease. But, being comfortable with yourself teaches you to interact with more equanimity toward others and not overreact because you feel judged. It helps you proactively choose what is good for you.

Knowing who you are is the ultimate freedom. Often people feel they are free but are really programmed by their environment. They might feel they make decisions for themselves but end up choosing professions, mates, or lifestyles based on what their parents favor. It's hard to be truly free unless you know who you are.

Take my word for it—it's not always comfortable to have this freedom. People will blame you for being rebellious when your personal truth is not in line with what they perceive as societal norms. Because no one wants to be alone, it's often too difficult to stand your ground. People will relentlessly urge you to do what they think is right, especially your family. Don't get divorced, don't move away, don't leave your job.

---

46   Daniel Goleman, "What Makes a Leader?" *Harvard Business Review*, January 2004.

Although this comes from love and a desire to protect you or prevent you from making mistakes, it is not always what's best for you. How do you separate your personal need for fulfillment from your family's desires? Be brave. In the long run, they will acknowledge that you made the right choice and may even join you in their exploration.

DIGITAL IDENTITY

Before you put effort into an online digital identity, make sure it is based on who you are and what you want to share. Your digital persona is a reflection showcasing what you want the world to see. Before you invest hours developing a digital facade that you share with others, you need to focus on your inner self. Once you have a better understanding of who you are and why you need a digital identity, you will be more confident about what to post and what not to share.

Using loads of energy to create an outer identity is cosmetic, like plastic surgery. But if you don't shine from the inside, it's just a shell. This reminds me of companies that launch an entire marketing campaign without first establishing their core vision. Without a focused brand identity, a company's marketing campaign is worthless. No one knows this better than brands like Apple, Nike, or Disney—who can communicate in one line who they are and what they're about.

DIFFERENTIATING BETWEEN LABELS
AND IDENTITY

Your identity is a conglomerate of factors, qualities, beliefs, and values that distinguish you from other people. You don't want to make the mistake of defining yourself based on specific physical characteristics or lifestyle choices. These are just labels. They're limited to describing one aspect of your identity. Labels like introvert, right-wing, animal-lover, musician, executive, vegan, pacifist, globalist, or atheist help explain some of your personality characteristics to others—but they don't define who you are. That said, we all find comfort in being part of some bigger group.

As human beings, we have a need to belong to groups. As eloquently expressed by Amy Chua: "We crave bonds and attachments, which is why we love clubs, teams, fraternities, family. These group identities are not national, but ethnic, regional, religious, sectarian, or clan based."[47] But defining what you belong to is not the same as defining who you are. The exploration might be the same but the results are a little bit different.

Another aspect that makes today's society overwhelming is that there are so many thousands of these new labels. Although labels might provide some sense of belonging, they can't substitute for the internal process a person has to go through to cultivate their individual identity and discover

47   Amy Chua, *Political Tribes*, (London: Penguin Press, 2018).

their collective identity and belonging. Because these labels are not rooted in your identity, they will work on a superficial level for a while, but be rendered obsolete later on.

A simplistic example would be a spirited young child who is crazy about soccer. Because he's a fan, he idolizes David Beckham. When he moves to a new school and his best friend convinces him to switch to basketball, David Beckham no longer works as a role model. If we could teach him to think about what in David Beckham impressed him so much—perhaps his passion for the sport, his leadership skills, or focus on training—we could give the child a tool to go deeper. Wouldn't it be amazing if this young boy would say, "I want to be like David Beckham because of his dedication to improve every day?" The process of asking questions can serve as a guide to navigating the internet or new social trends. Asking himself about the attraction to certain sub-identities will help this child develop or support his personality, instead of substituting each label with some other superficial tag. Otherwise, today it's David Beckham, tomorrow it's Michael Jordan, the next day it's the YouTuber who wrote a one-hit-wonder. This same child will eventually watch and follow his role models' political views, but he won't understand why he's following them. He will remain confused—and that's exactly how many of us feel right now.

MULTICULTURALISM AND ITS IMPACT
ON IDENTITY

There is a long liberal tradition of downplaying the importance of tribal identity. Many intellectuals insist that we are all the same and all motivated by the drive to succeed economically; we are all rational beings. Although this might sound logical, more and more research studies in behavioral economics, such as those by Nobel Prize winner Daniel Kahneman and Amos Tversky[48], have proved that we do not necessarily behave rationally. Sometimes liberal views ignore the realities of human nature. We have a need to be part of something bigger and we can't deny where we come from. Only then can we be truly liberal and accepting of others.

When mainstream politicians neglect this part of people's identity and don't leave room for its expression, the extremists end up being the only ones shouting about how everyone is different. This has led to an increase in their popularity and the result is a rise in nationalism and violence. We must leave room for people to embrace and celebrate cultural identities.

The failed effort by the Soviet Union to create a single persona for all citizens is a perfect example of why a uniform (de

---

48   Kahneman, D., & Tversky, A. (1979). Prospect theory: An analysis of decision under risk. *Econometrica, 47*, 263-291.

facto multicultural) society cannot work.[49] The term *Homo Sovieticus* (Latin for "Soviet Man") was coined by Mikhail Heller to describe what was to be the next evolutionary level of humanity, thanks to the success of Marxism.[50] Ultimately, this idea proved disastrous and the real Homo Sovieticus more closely resembled the person described by Lev Gudkov and Eva Hartog in their *Moscow Times* article: "Sovyetsky chelovek (Soviet man) is the archetype of a person born in and shaped by a totalitarian regime. Life in repressive conditions has made him crafty and skilled at doublethink. He knows how to bypass the authorities' demands while simultaneously maintaining informal and corrupt relations with them."[51] Gudkov was one of the first people to take public opinion polls in Russia once the Iron Curtain fell. His survey summed up the repercussions of the attempted, homogeneous communist identity. Soviet citizens pretended to work and pretended to care, but their real interest lay only in their home and family. They felt they had no power and mistrusted everyone but those closest to their family, and expected nothing good from anyone else. Because people felt they had no decision-making power, they did not feel responsible for the outcome and did not care.

49　"Homo Sovieticus," *Wikipedia*, last modified April 20, 2019, https://en.wikipedia.org/wiki/Homo_Sovieticus

50　Mikhail Heller, *Cogs in the Wheel: The Formation of Soviet Man*, (New York: Alfred A. Knopf, 1988).

51　Eva Hartog and Lev Gudkov, "The Evolution of Homo Sovieticus to Putin's Man," *The Moscow Times*, October 13, 2017, https://themoscowtimes.com/articles/the-evolution-of-homo-sovieticus-to-putins-man-59189

TAKING FULL RESPONSIBILITY FOR YOUR LIFE

> *Everything can be taken from a man but one thing: the last of the human freedoms—to choose one's attitude in any given set of circumstances, to choose one's own way.*

— **Viktor E. Frankl**

We are born with our genetic load, on top of which we are influenced by external forces from our upbringing, lifestyle choices, experiences, and more. On top of these forces, there are the "stories" that we are taught about what is good or not good, what is doable, and what lies beyond our reach. Taking full responsibility for your life means learning to peel away these tales. It's about stopping and analyzing how you make decisions and where you make them from. Not everything you want to do will be acceptable to others. That doesn't mean it's wrong. It's a matter of learning who you are, as opposed to who the world says you should be.

Dr. Hodaya Oliel, twenty-eight-years-old from Ashdod, is a perfect example of ignoring what others feel is the norm. At the 2019 Independence Day ceremony in Israel, she was one of fifteen people chosen to light a torch and deeply touched everyone in the audience. Despite being diagnosed with cerebral palsy as a child, she completed medical school at the Technion - Israel Institute of Technology and is now starting her residency at the Kaplan Medical Center. Born three months prematurely, weighing less than a kilogram, she spent many years of her childhood in and out of hospitals. This was when she began to dream of becoming a doctor.

Beyond her obvious intelligence, Hodaya is an outstanding symbol of strength, courage, persistence, and, above all, taking responsibility. She never would have finished medical school or gotten so far in life had she chosen to be a victim of her circumstances or given up responsibility for her life.

If you want to more efficiently direct your life's energy—something we never have enough of—you need to eliminate the stress caused by worry and frustration. The way to do that is by taking responsibility. In a *Harvard Business Review* article, John Coleman equates taking responsibility with taking ownership of your actions. This occurs when you start believing that you are personally accountable for the outcome of a situation. You did not always cause the situation and cannot always control it—but you own the ability and have the choice to take action and effect change. Start by looking forward at what can be or what needs to be done—instead of backward at what or who is at fault. I agree with Coleman's statement: "Fixating on blame delays taking corrective action and inhibits learning. Focusing on responsibility offers a sense of peace."[52] Once you feel that you are responsible, you stop worrying and waiting for someone else to help or act. You begin thinking about and seeking out new solutions that will change what is going on. Very often, this action not only helps you—it can inspire and benefit others in similar situations.

---

52 John Coleman, "Take Ownership of Your Actions by Taking Responsibility," *Harvard Business Review,* August 30, 2012, https://hbr.org/2012/08/take-ownership-of-your-actions

When you are in charge, less emotional and physical energy is spent on going nowhere. When you continue those boring dinners with friends every Thursday evening simply because you've done it for so many years, you are frittering away your life's energy. Do you enjoy this dinner or do you spend the following morning detoxing? Has the tradition run its course? Are you sitting with people while you wish you were home reading instead? Use your energy to look inside and ask yourself the difficult questions about whether this is what you really enjoy doing. Or perhaps face the fact that you are no longer interested. It was great fun for a while and now it's time to move on. You get to make the rules.

When you take responsibility, you make the choice—whether it has to do with career moves, family, marriage, household chores, where you live, or how you live. This is the case both outside your home and family and within. For example, my husband looks forward to having a traditional Shabbat dinner every Friday night, including lovely rituals with wine, candles, and prayers. While I have enormous gratitude for the strength I get from my Jewish roots and the wisdom of the Jewish people, that doesn't mean I feel the need to observe all the traditions. People often ask me: "How do you make it work so that each person has what they need but you lead a life together?" It's easiest to reconcile different perspectives through an open discussion, where each person says what is important to them and a decision is made together. It was my decision to hold a traditional dinner every Friday night. I chose to do this out of love and respect for my husband. Not as a compromise, but as a choice that is important for our life together. If I did this because it was his choice and I didn't want him to be upset, I would end up feeling frustrated because I disregarded my own needs.

CONNECTING TO WHAT WILL NOT CHANGE: YOUR PEOPLE

One of my missions in life is to help connect people to their collective identity, so they can become stronger and more resilient. From the time I was thirteen when I started the Jewish school and met a group of people who were similar to me, I understood how essential it is to feel part of a group of like-minded peers and extended family.

When I stepped into the role of chairperson for the Museum of the Jewish People in Tel Aviv, it was a chance to practice what I preach. For me, the museum is both a proof of concept and a thriving test case for the formula of how to be stronger by connecting to your people. The museum connects Jewish people to their roots and strengthens their personal and collective identity. It does this by telling the story of the Jewish people and the essence of the Jewish culture and faith while presenting the contributions made to humanity by world Jewry. People can relate to their amazing roots through exhibits on a wide range of topics, which run from the creativity of Bob Dylan to the humor of Hollywood and the racial issues of the Ethiopian community. Our goal is to provide an entry point for each person to find their connection to the story through ideas that matter to them.

Together with the museum's talented staff, I enjoy applying an entrepreneurial outlook to extend the experience so it includes even more engaging content. Although this specific museum is focused on the Jewish people, I see it as an effective model for ways to deepen and strengthen the collective identity of any people. Channeling my energy into building and shaping the museum works much better than wasting it feeling the world is in chaos, reading about conspiracy theories, and blaming "others" for what is wrong.

Jewish history is rife with stories of mysticism, bravery, and tradition. The museum allows anyone to gain knowledge—fewer myths, more facts. It goes beyond learning about historical incidents or traditional food and dress. It's the ongoing story of a people—past, present, and future. The museum also has an education center that serves as a gathering place for discourse, engagement, and learning for individuals, families, communities, and organizations from Israel and around the world.

Our aim is to educate all Jewish people about their roots and help them realize what an amazing family they belong to. One example of how we accomplish this is an initiative called "My Family Story," an annual competition that is already in its twenty-fourth year. Each child has a conversation with their family members to learn what life was like in the past—whether through discussions with grandparents or other family connections. The children then create an artistic expression of how they envision this Jewish way of life. These works of art are sent to the museum from hundreds of thousands of people around the world. The judges select the best works, which are displayed in a special section of the museum.

This goes hand in hand with a project that every Israeli child in middle school has to complete in order to explore their roots. The students interview their parents, grandparents, aunts, and uncles and write down the stories of their background and family trees. Why not have every teenager around the world engage in something similar to help them learn about their people? A simple activity that works well is having students at school or people at work each bring a traditional dish from their people to share at a collective breakfast. Imagine a classroom or boardroom with an enticing buffet of French, Scottish, Japanese, Spanish, and Indian delicacies! Researching and sharing different ethnic holiday traditions, music, or movies is another fun way to feel pride in your personal or collective identity.

Another example from the museum is an exhibition called *Heroes*, in which visitors become acquainted with different types of Jewish heroes throughout history. This includes scientists, intellectuals, leaders, revolutionaries, cultural figures, athletes, and more—since success has many different faces. These heroes inspire children, and their parents, to ask who is truly brave and to identify their own personal heroes and role models. What if there was a similar museum in Rome celebrating Italian heroes, a similar one in Kenya, and another in Norway? You get the idea.

The museum is a way to ignite people's curiosity, so they start asking questions about themselves.

CHAPTER 5

Enjoying a bold spirit of adventure

ACQUIRING NEW SKILLS

Once you realize that it is within your power to make choices, the opportunities for new knowledge, attitudes, and action will become more apparent. When you are ready to be proactive and scoop them up, you will begin exercising your "change muscle." Once you strengthen this muscle, the new brings with it excitement and the celebration of rich experiences.

I want to share some practical directions that really helped me exercise my change muscle. No doubt, you will also have a few ideas that can accomplish similar goals. There are many experts, courses, books, and distinguished schools that can provide you with more details and proper training in these areas.

LEARN A NEW LANGUAGE

When immigrants learn the new language of their host country, it involves much more than just the language itself. It's about learning new societal codes and opening up to the unfamiliar. Every country has expressions that reflect the nation and its culture. For example, executives in the US have a long history of using baseball references as part of their corporate culture. What are our "big bets" for this year? This one is a "game-changer," so let's "keep your eye on the ball." In Russia, there is no expression for "take your time;" it simply doesn't exist in an ideology where you're one of many and don't have "your own time." In Britain, along with sports idioms like those in the US, you are likely to hear expressions such as "chockablock" or "we were just faffing about."

By learning these expressions and another language, you expand your horizons, boost your ability to connect with people, and appreciate that people are different. You learn about the identity of other peoples and it helps you to question your own. All this opens up your brain so you can be more comfortable in the world.

Learning another language is a fabulous way to step outside of your comfort zone. Beyond the practical benefits of being able to communicate with more people, scientists have discovered that being bilingual can have an astonishing effect on your brain. Research shows that it can improve cognitive skills not related to language and even help defend against dementia in old age.

In a *New York Times* article on "Why Bilinguals Are Smarter," Yudhijit Bhattacharjee explained that: "The collective evidence from a number of such studies suggests that the bilingual experience improves the brain's so-called executive *cognitive reserve - cerebral (instrument)*

function—a command system that directs the attention processes that we use for planning, solving problems and performing various other mentally demanding tasks."[53]

I was fascinated to learn how being bilingual can not only benefit children as they learn to speak but also adults as they age. First of all, researchers see increases in the volume of "gray matter" in the brain of bilingual people. The brain is made up of cells called neurons, each of which has a cell body and little branching connections called dendrites. Our gray matter refers to how many cell bodies and dendrites there are. Results show that the bilingual experience makes gray matter denser, so you have more cells—in other words, a healthier brain.

Naturally, everyone should go all out when it comes to learning the official language of their country. Otherwise, you can end up being isolated in a small community that lives in somewhat a parallel universe. But even native citizens should make it a point to learn a second language. English is ranked as number one in importance outside of Chinese, and Spanish comes next if you want to live more easily in the global village.[54] According to an estimate by the British Council English is spoken by some 1.75 billion

53   Yudhijit Bhattacharjee, "Why Bilinguals are Smarter," *The New York Times*, March 17, 2012, https://www.nytimes.com/2012/03/18/opinion/sunday/the-benefits-of-bilingualism.html?_r=0

54   "10 Most Important Business Languages in Global Market," *The Startup*, October 4, 2018, https://medium.com/swlh/10-most-important-business-languages-in-global-market-17b49b7cf2d2

people worldwide as their first or second language—that's about twenty percent of the world's population.[55] English is sometimes called the "operating system" of the global economic conversation being conducted by thought leaders and decision-makers.

Knowing another language makes you more flexible and open-minded because you end up learning another culture, not just another language. Once you use the new language, you will be amazed at the feeling of confidence it can inspire. Being more confident is the gateway to becoming more receptive to new ideas, more versatile, and more adaptable.

MOVE TO CRITICAL THINKING

One of the side effects of the current era is that we are being bombarded with information. We open our eyes in the morning and reach for our phones or laptops. And it's often the last thing we check before falling asleep. (I've even heard of people who text in their sleep.) It's usually helpful to go on a "diet" from Facebook or dial down the frequency you check for news. But, for most of us, shutting everything down is not an option. Learning to examine and filter what we ingest has become an essential skill. We have to learn it, sharpen it, and continuously adapt it to new concerns—like fake news or promoted material that is dressed up as fact.

---

55   The British Council, *The English Effect*, (London: British Council, 2013), https://www.britishcouncil.org/sites/default/files/english-effect-report-v2.pdf

People's opinions matter, but not all opinions are based on fact. It has become vital to stop, listen, breathe, and think before you believe something and rely on someone else's viewpoint. There is no rule that says someone else's opinion is more valuable than your own instinct. Take the time to seek out the source and think about why the source published or disclosed this information at this point in time. Remember, just because a politician tweeted something, that doesn't make it true. If a huge number of people share it on Facebook and are talking about it, that doesn't make it accurate or authentic. It's time to develop your own sense of critical thinking.

The term "critical thinking" refers to the process of trying to remove subjectivity by thoughtfully analyzing and questioning the information we receive—from all sources. Lee Watanabe-Crockett summed it up nicely: "It's more than just thinking clearly or rationally; it's about thinking independently. Critically thinking about something means taking the time to formulate your own opinion and draw your own conclusions—no matter what others are saying."[56]

When you make a judgement call, solve a problem, or make an important decision, you are using the skills of critical thinking. By analyzing, evaluating, and connecting new ideas to what we already know, we can cut down on the risk

---

56   Lee Watanabe-Crockett, "12 Strong Strategies for Effectively Teaching Critical Thinking Skills," *Wabisabi Learning*, May 6, 2019, https://globaldigitalcitizen.org/12-strategies-teaching-critical-thinking-skills

of believing or acting on false information.

I feel extremely passionate about the need to teach this skill to young students. Developing the courage to think for themselves and learning how to abandon group-think are skills that should be taught from a young age. How to critically process information, and either accept it or reject it, can be more valuable in the long run than much of the material emphasized during the crucial years of school. Just as an example, more countries could look to the Finnish educational system where they teach and prioritize critical thinking skills by meshing them with the subjects taught. Educators should invite the students to ask questions, understand what is evidence-based, come up with their own interpretations and insights, apply what they learn, and invent. Today's education has to teach students to do much more than learn and recall if they are to thrive.

DEVELOP A BEGINNER'S MIND—BECOME A LIFELONG LEARNER

If your mind is empty, it is always ready for anything; it is open to everything. In the beginner's mind there are many possibilities; in the expert's mind there are few.

— **Zen teacher Shunryu Suzuki**

Because our life expectancy has extended dramatically, and we are far more active for many more years, it's vital that we continue learning all the time. One way to do this is to develop a beginner's mind.

A beginner's mind is clear. It has no preconceived ideas or rules. It's waiting to be filled, willing to learn, and open to new discoveries. Say someone asks you to draw a house. For most of us, the first image that comes to mind is the classic square with a triangle on top, perhaps adding two windows and a door. A beginner's mind can picture a house as an igloo, a boat, or even a bird's nest.

Like its name, the beginner's mindset refers to being open and receptive, no matter how expert you become on a subject.[57] Being open and receptive can start with how you judge others. This is something you can practice whenever you talk to another person, dropping your ideas of how they should act, and, instead, emptying your mind and seeing them as they are. No judgment. No threat from their opinions or views.

Alongside being open-minded and ready to learn, try to turn up the dial on your curiosity. Be self-motivated. Let yourself be delighted by new discoveries, different ways to approach problems, or unique approaches to life.

In his book *The Farther Reaches of Human Nature*, Abraham Maslow brings up a similar notion. He found creative people surrender themselves to a kind of innocence of the mind.[58]

---

57 Karson McGinley, "8 Tips for Cultivating a Beginner's Mind," *The Chopra Center*, n.d., https://chopra.com/articles/8-tips-for-cultivating-a-beginners-mind

58 https://scottjeffrey.com/beginners-mind/#What_is_a_Beginners_Mind

Maslow writes: "They are variously described as being naked in the situation, guileless ... without 'shoulds' or 'oughts,' without fashions, fads, dogmas, habits, or other pictures-in-the-head of what is proper, normal, 'right,' as being ready to receive whatever happens to be the case without surprise, shock, indignation, or denial."

If you can let go of expectations and preconceived ideas, you can observe and explore the "now" with a fresh and creative approach—like a beginner.

In *The Oxford Handbook of Lifelong Learning*, Manuel London notes that learning is all about change, and change drives learning: the two are inevitable and go hand in glove.[59] Change is opportunity—whether at work, in relationships, or in other areas of life. Being open to the new—without pre-judging—is an opportunity to learn new skills, new capabilities, and to find meaning. It also gives you the chance to make a difference and influence the world around you.

59 Manuel London, ed., *The Oxford Handbook of Lifelong* Learning, (Oxford: Oxford Library of Psychology, 2011), www.oxfordhandbooks.com/view/10.1093/oxfordhb/9780195390483.001.0001/oxfordhb-9780195390483-e-001

EPILOGUE

Let's build a new world

So how do you spark a new way of looking at the world and addressing it in a positive, resilient way? We live in an era of unprecedented disruption in which old identities simply don't work anymore. To face the new, ever-changing world, it's important to ignite a continuous process of understanding who you are, where you belong, and what is right for you. One way to do this is by (1) Connecting to your roots, (2) Looking at immigrants as a model for how to develop internal resources, and (3) Taking responsibility for your choices and where you are in life.

GET ROOTED

The simplest way to start is by building strong healthy roots. Once these roots are firmly in place, the road to developing a solid personal identity becomes more straightforward; thinking and examining what choices are the right ones for you becomes more natural. The next step, connecting to your people, will complement this firm foundation with a strong feeling of belonging. Now you can be both rooted and resilient.

TAKE A LESSON FROM IMMIGRANTS

Many of us perceive immigrants, newcomers, and minorities as people who lack resources and are disadvantaged. In reality, their lack of external resources compels them to develop internal strength. We've discussed numerous examples showing how they manage to triumph over obstacles and build successful lives in their new countries. We should all be asking ourselves the same questions these immigrants ask about what to leave behind and what new ideas and attitudes to adopt. Life circumstances forced many of them to stop living on autopilot and to start questioning their every action. You can do it too.

ACCEPT RESPONSIBILITY

Decide to take responsibility for what you make of your life no matter how tough things get, and stop blaming other people or circumstances for your failures. When you ask questions and take responsibility for your answers you are in healthy control and at ease with your life. You are no longer a victim and the environment does not dictate your success. You feel solid and secure, less intimidated by others. Like a tree with strong roots, you are grounded, resilient, and ready to branch up and out.

FORGING THE FUTURE BY THINKING BIGGER

Perhaps by now, you are starting to believe that it's possible to enjoy life and feel safer in our fast-changing world.

Disruption and transformation lead to new opportunities.

It is time to stop wasting energy yearning for the past. The old world is not coming back—we have a new one to build. Can you imagine what society would be like if school teachers taught us to take responsibility for our life, connect to our roots, and develop a strong sense of belonging? So let's stop blaming and complaining and instead, ask ourselves what choices we can make that will lead to a more meaningful life. Let's go build a new world!

Made in the USA
Coppell, TX
07 October 2020

39412669R00072